Supporting Pupils on the Autism Spectrum in Secondary Schools

Written to meet the needs of teaching assistants and learning support assistants, this book provides a practical toolkit for supporting students on the autism spectrum in mainstream secondary schools.

The book offers a clear, jargon-free explanation of autism spectrum conditions and examines the difficulties arising from these conditions and how they can impact on students' learning. Addressing issues that arise on a daily basis, it is full of practical advice and strategies for supporting students socially and academically across all areas of the curriculum. Features include:

- templates to scaffold students' comprehension and learning in different subject areas;
- forms to help with information collection and evaluation;
- advice on supporting students through examinations;
- examples and case studies to illustrate how the strategies described work in practice.

Packed with photocopiable resources that can be adapted to suit individual students' needs, this book is essential reading for teaching assistants who want to help their students on the autism spectrum to reach their full potential.

Cary Canavan is a Consultant in Autism specializing in Asperger Syndrome. She offers training, advice and support for those teaching and employing young people with AS.

Supporting Pupils on the Autism Spectrum in Secondary Schools

A Practical Guide for Teaching Assistants

Cary Canavan

Routledge
Taylor & Francis Group

LONDON AND NEW YORK

First published 2015
by Routledge
2 Park Square, Milton Park, Abingdon, Oxon OX14 4RN

and by Routledge
711 Third Avenue, New York, NY 10017

Routledge is an imprint of the Taylor & Francis Group, an informa business

British Library Cataloguing in Publication Data
A catalogue record for this book is available from the British Library

Library of Congress Cataloging in Publication Data
Canavan, Carolyn.
Supporting pupils on the autism spectrum in secondary schools : a practical guide for teaching assistants / Cary Canavan.
pages cm
1. Autistic children--Education (Secondary) 2. Teachers' assistants--Handbooks, manuals, etc. I. Title.
LC4717.C36 2014
371.9--dc23
2014019038

ISBN: 978-1-138-78334-8 (hbk)
ISBN: 978-1-138-78335-5 (pbk)
ISBN: 978-1-315-76872-4 (ebk)

Typeset in Helvetica
by Saxon Graphics Ltd, Derby

Printed and bound in Great Britain by CPI Group (UK) Ltd, Croydon, CR0 4YY

This book is dedicated to pupils on the autism spectrum who go to mainstream schools, and the staff who support them. A special mention of the boys and girls who were the inspiration for this book, I loved working with you all. They were the most rewarding years of my career.

Contents

Foreword

This is a much-needed book, which covers a wide range of issues that affect young people with Asperger Syndrome accessing mainstream education. It provides focused guidance on strategies that may be useful not only to teaching assistants and other staff who support in class, but also to the wider staff team. It is written in language that is accessible to those who may have little knowledge and experience of autism or specialist teaching techniques, and it gives clear examples of approaches that could really help in an educational setting. It starts from the perspective that most young people with Asperger Syndrome suffer from huge levels of anxiety and that the world can be a very confusing place for them. This singular notion is possibly the most profound and important fact in understanding and supporting individuals in an effective, pro-active and positive manner.

The prevalence of autism has seen a dramatic rise in the past 10 years and many pupils with Asperger Syndrome are now educated in a mainstream setting and units in mainstream schools. Many do not have a formal diagnosis, or they receive late diagnosis, and often their needs are not understood by staff who can interpret their presentation as 'difficult' and 'non-compliant'. Their unique style of learning can sit uncomfortably with traditional teaching methods and without an underpinning knowledge of the neurological and psychological differences, these young people can struggle to engage in a coherent manner. The hope is that staff can use the ideas, information and resources in this book to enable pupils with Asperger Syndrome to have a much more positive experience in school and use their unique talents to enhance their ability to gain skills and knowledge and to apply these in a flexible and successful manner.

Many teaching assistants take on the role with little or no formal training and are often left to manage the most complex pupils in the school. It may also be the case that the teacher has received little if any training to manage these young people.

The book begins with a moving outline of the strengths that a young person with Asperger Syndrome may have and it sets the scene for working with these very special assets, which can signpost staff in the development of programmes and styles of teaching that may be successful. It is only with an understanding of the idiosyncratic learning styles that one can begin to think creatively about the most appropriate curriculum, environment and support. The book is clear that a 'one size fits all model' is unlikely to be successful and that staff need to understand why young people with Asperger Syndrome need a differentiated approach to access learning that is functional and meaningful. The positive nature of the way that this is explained and explored makes the process of understanding one that the reader feels empowered and enthusiastic to engage with.

The section on 'difficult parents' is humbling but also informative as to the impact that effective educational environments can have not just on the pupil but on the whole family, and this is often ignored. Parents can be a huge source of information about their child, and the value of engaging with parents is clearly outlined, especially in developing a supportive transition package. If staff can get this crucial step right then it is much more likely that the placement will succeed.

A huge strength of the book is the templates provided to collate information and make sure that everybody who comes into contact with the pupil will have easily accessible information that will help them to understand the best way of engaging with them, and how to do this in a non-threatening manner.

In recent years there has been a plethora of research and ideas about how sensory issues can affect people with autism. Cary gives some examples of how to identify these and reduce the impact of poor sensory modulation. She offers a clear pathway as to how to work most effectively with environments, and strategies that can be employed to reduce or ameliorate the stress that they can cause. It is vital that staff understand that this single issue can have a profound effect on learning and an increase in anxiety. The strategies offered are sensible and achievable in a mainstream setting without the need for expensive equipment or intrusive modification to the school environment. It is of note that Cary also suggests pupils need to be given the tools to self-modulate their own responses, rather than just relying on others to manage this for them. However, the checklist also acts as a valuable aide memoire to staff in defining the issues and giving practical solutions to work with.

Cary originally designed the lesson templates for her own use whilst teaching English to pupils with Asperger Syndrome and they proved to be extremely successful. They have been modified and developed over a period of time and offer a design that builds on key concepts leading to a more in-depth understanding of the topic. This focus on detail and support led a number of students to gain high GCSE grades but, more importantly, gave students a meaningful insight into the text and a way of working that was logical, comfortable and made sense to them.

One of the biggest problems a mainstream setting can face is effectively managing and understanding behaviour, particularly when strategies have not been successful. The advice given starts at the point before this happens, and suggests some simple, yet highly effective, responses to this. There are also some excellent examples given of how to safely manage behaviour when a pupil has lost control, as well as an extremely informative section on recovery and reflection. It also outlines the very important issue of keeping detailed records of incidents so that patterns and triggers can be spotted.

No two pupils with autism will have the same presentation and because of this it is imperative that staff are able to profile and collate specific information so that the programmes developed are reflective of both strengths and areas of likely difficulty. Some pupils may present with skills that appear to be in line with their peers; however, with knowledge and understanding of the difference in perception, it may be that underpinning skills require further consolidation. If this is not forthcoming the pupil can plateau and struggle to make further progress. Recovery programmes are unlikely to be helpful, as this problem is due to a difference in processing rather than a delay.

There have been many books written that highlight the core features of autism but few offer practical solutions to this in a user-friendly format. This book is effective as a whole approach but also works as a reference book that can be used in sections to provide practical advice in specific areas. The book identifies areas of potential stress and gives suggestions that may be useful in addressing these.

This book is long overdue and will be a valuable tool for all mainstream settings working with pupils with Asperger Syndrome. It demonstrates the evaluation of theoretical ideas and offers a working model that can be translated into good classroom practice. It is a must for any school staff room.

Allison Hope-West
Autism Director, Priory Group

How to use this book

The book is split into three parts:

Part One is about Asperger Syndrome: the basic physiology, in layman's terms, and how it can impact upon a person's life, together with a brief history of the condition.

Part Two deals with how the school's social and physical environment can impact upon the pupil's behaviour and how to manage it. It is very important to prepare for the pupil before he or she arrives. This section deals with laying down the foundations for a smooth transition from primary to secondary school; how to react in a crisis and how to avoid one altogether.

Part Three's chapters relate to specific subject areas, the difficulties they present and strategies, including photocopiable templates, for you to use to support your target pupils across the curriculum.

I hope that when you put any of the strategies into practice you will understand why it may be of benefit to the pupil on the autism spectrum. The book builds upon the need for consistency and clear instructions to support the pupil across the curriculum by reducing the number of different ways to do the same thing and maintaining clarity of language so that the pupil understands exactly what is expected of them.

Most chapters contain an explanation on how the condition, as a neurological developmental disorder, affects the topic, be it behaviour or learning. This is followed by a discussion, practical advice, a detailed description of strategies, and templates to enable you to support them effectively in lessons. I have also discussed GCSE examinations and how the pupil may be supported through this process to effect a positive outcome in examinations.

There is a comprehensive reading list of books and website addresses exploring the issues in greater depth at the end of each topic chapter, and all references are to be found in the Bibliography at the end. I have read all the books and chosen them for their usefulness and readability. The most interesting and insightful are those written by people on the spectrum, and these are marked with an asterisk.

Autism is a heterogeneous condition. This means that no two people with the condition are the same. A strategy or intervention that works with one child may not work with another. Therefore it is vital for you to learn about each individual and how you may support them effectively in school. Find out about their unique, autistic operating system: AutOS.

Autism is also largely a hidden condition. The pupil with a diagnosis of an autism spectrum condition or Asperger Syndrome, whether they have a statement of special educational need or not, has several basic needs and these are best met by putting together an Individual Education Plan, which should include the following principles:

1 Maintain consistency at all times – avoid changes when possible.
2 Prepare for any changes – staff, room, timetable, groups – well in advance.
3 Have strategies in place from the start, which all staff dealing with the pupil apply without deviation.

4   Expectations of behaviour and working practices should be consistent from lesson to lesson, room to room, staff member to staff member.

If the pupil knows what is expected of them, they can meet those needs and feel safe and competent. Change leads to confusion, fear and has a profound effect upon the pupil's self-esteem. **Knowledge** of the impact of autism, **Understanding** of the pupil's needs and **Tolerance** and a genuine regard for the individual will enable you to support them to do the best they can. They will not disappoint you.

Accept   ≈   Respect   ≈   Protect

Note on the terminology used in this book

According to the National Autistic Society (NAS): 'The term "autism" is used to describe all diagnoses on the autism spectrum including classic autism, Asperger Syndrome and high-functioning autism.'

Recently, the American Psychiatric Association dropped Asperger Syndrome in favour of the term Autism Spectrum Disorder from the fifth edition of their *Diagnostic Statistical Manual* (DSM-5) to cover the full spectrum of autism.

However, Asperger Syndrome is still classified as a separate term by the NAS, which is a primary resource here in the UK; so I use the term Asperger Syndrome (AS) and Autism Spectrum Conditions (ASC) interchangeably throughout the book.

Introduction

Staff supporting pupils on the autism spectrum in mainstream secondary schools are very special people. They are interpreters, guardians and advocates. This is for you. I hope the practical strategies and templates in this book will help you support your pupils and teachers across a range of subjects.

I am an ex-English teacher with Special Educational Needs (SEN) teaching experience in primary and secondary schools. My son was diagnosed with Asperger Syndrome (AS) at the age of 13. When I realized he was autistic, two years before he was diagnosed, I resolved to learn as much as I could about the condition (this will be a lifetime project). While studying for my master's degree in autism at the University of Birmingham, I took a job as a teaching assistant (TA) in a mainstream, secondary school supporting pupils with AS. The strategies I used were the beginning of this book.

At least 1 in 100 children are diagnosed with an ASC and 71 per cent of these are now educated in mainstream schools. However, only 22 per cent of teachers have been trained specifically in ASCs, and typically for only 1–4 hours. Ideally, each school should have an autism base with specially trained support staff to support the pupils on the spectrum, and a continuous programme of training for all teachers in ASCs.

The reality is that the Asperkid is another pupil on the SEN register and supported or not by members of the SEN team, who may or may not have been trained or understand the condition and its impact on learning and behaviour. However, in my experience, TAs are going on the courses, attending local authority training and sometimes know more about AS than teachers.

Using the square peg (person with AS) round peg (neuro-typical person: NT) analogy: mainstream schools have lots of round holes; some may be different sizes to accommodate the broad range of round pegs, but essentially they are all round holes. Square pegs do not fit into round holes, unless you shave off the corners and knock them in. When you do this, you damage the square peg. It may look round but it isn't. If you have square pegs, make some square holes into which they can fit easily or, at the very least, make the round holes larger.

Many educators advocate the latter, believing that children with AS need to be de-sensitized and learn how to fit into the NT (non-autistic) world. Autistic children will become autistic adults. They may learn how to manage themselves but that only works in an autism-friendly environment. They still suffer extreme stress and can meltdown or shutdown when overloaded. This doesn't change whether they are aged 14 or 40.

The purpose of this book is to explain, in layman's terms, why pupils with AS have difficulties with learning and social skills and display idiosyncratic behaviours. Issues are discussed, followed by detailed advice, strategies and the tools to implement them. These are not exhaustive and I hope that you will read some of the recommended texts and develop your own strategies, tailoring them to the needs of the individual pupil you work with.

I hope that by the time you finish this book and are practised in using the strategies, the support you give them will be underpinned by an understanding of why the child with AS behaves this way, the difficulties they face and how you might support them and develop your own strategies and resources appropriate to the individual child.

Finally, I would just like to say thank you for reading this book. I infer from this that you are interested in children like my son, and care enough to seek ways to help them achieve the best they can. Our children quite literally change the world, for all their difficulties.

Part One

1 Strengths of individuals with Asperger Syndrome

Before I talk about their difficulties, I would like to write about some of their strengths:

- The individual with AS is loyal and will persevere with a friendship, even if let down. They are socially optimistic.
- They are free from prejudice and accept people at face value.
- Contrary to popular belief, they are very empathic and may surprise you with their insight. (They just don't know what to do about another person's feelings.)
- They will tell you what they really feel and think about something rather than what they think you want to hear.
- When they ask a question – they want the honest answer to it. There is no hidden motive behind it.
- They will tell the truth even if it means getting themselves into trouble.
- They rarely do something they know to be wrong, even when pressured.
- They have a strong sense of justice and neither fear nor favour.
- Their humour can be unique and unconventional.
- They love words, especially puns, and will use them to make up their own jokes.
- They want to co-operate but often don't know how.
- If they enjoy a sport, they will train hard to be the best and are particularly good at individual sports rather than team games.
- They have the ability to learn quickly and want to progress, especially if interested in the topic.
- When they start a task they want to do it perfectly.
- They have a good eye for detail and will pick up mistakes.
- If it interests them, they can concentrate on a single task for a very long period of time.
- When they are interested or motivated in a task they will persevere with an extraordinary determination to finish.
- Their long-term memory is good, especially for childhood experiences, facts, figures, dates and film dialogue or audio recordings.
- They are creative, often insightful, and can provide an original solution to a problem.
- Their spatial awareness can be quite remarkable – they are visual thinkers.
- They often have an encyclopaedic knowledge of their special interest.
- Of average or above average intelligence, they have the potential to go on to university.
- They often have an interest or a talent for something: design, Japanese, quantum physics, art, music or computing – find out what it is and nurture it.

2 Important things to know about Autism Spectrum Conditions

The Autism Spectrum covers a very broad range of Pervasive Developmental Disorders, which are lifelong neuro-physiological conditions:

- Classic Autism, also known as Kanner Syndrome or Low Functioning Autism;
- High Functioning Autism (HFA);
- Asperger Syndrome (AS);
- Semantic Pragmatic Disorder (SPD);
- Pathological Demand Avoidance Syndrome (PDA);
- Retts Syndrome;
- Tourette Syndrome;
- Pervasive Development Disorder Not Otherwise Specified (PDD-NOS) – this often develops into autism or AS later in life, or a child with autism may improve and be re-diagnosed with PDD-NOS.
  (See glossary for descriptions of each of these conditions.)

Most ASCs are hidden disabilities caused by differences in the formation of the brain and the way it responds to stimuli. This is backed up by research using *functional* Magnetic Resonance Imaging (fMRI) scans, which detect blood flow through the brain in response to a variety of stimuli. Consequently, our expectations of individuals with an ASC can sometimes be compared to asking a blind person to 'look at this' or a deaf person to 'listen'. This is why it is so important we understand the condition and appreciate the difficulties that those with it are confronted with on a daily basis.

The brains of people with Asperger Syndrome are larger than average neuro-typical brains and they have more white and grey matter. Grey matter is responsible for extracting and processing information from sensory organs (for example sight, sound, speech) and is involved in muscle control, memory and emotions. Various parts of the brain compare that information to what is in the memory and use the information to plan and execute behaviour. White matter carries information around the brain through electric and chemical activity but this is also disordered.

More recent research suggests that the autistic brain has more neural pathways to carry information round the brain but that they are not co-ordinated. Or that too much information comes into the brain than it is able to process, leading to overload. In order to function, people with autism use strategies to distract themselves from the stimuli which threaten to overwhelm them, leading to a display of idiosyncratic behaviours. Researchers concluded that this might explain the problems with attention: for example, too much information comes in through the visual system so that the person becomes distracted and shows less interest in social interaction. However, they also suggest that hyper-connectivity might also explain the islets of ability in mathematics and visual search or detailed focus processing.

Difficulties processing information

As a result of all these differences, people with an ASC have processing difficulties with social interaction; emotional recognition and regulation; impulse suppression; language processing – input and output; fine and gross motor skills; planning and organization; attention, short term memory, the ability to be flexible and sensory regulation. There may also be areas of profound ability in any subject area: not just science or maths but also music or art.

To use a metaphor to illustrate the problem:

1 The typical brain is like a fast road network. Information coming in at A goes to B by travelling along the neural pathways. Like a car travelling along the motorways, the information gets to its destination without any fuss.

2 The autistic brain is different. Information coming in at A goes to B, but it takes longer because of the differences in the brain, like a car going from A to B along b roads. It may even get lost and end up at the seaside (C) for a holiday and turn up at its original destination weeks or even months later.

   With the uneven distribution of grey and white matter, and the low levels of chemical neurotransmitters to push inhibitory messages across the synapses (joints), it may even be a more arduous journey with traffic jams and detours. The synapses may even be broken in some places so that processing is severely impaired and takes much longer.

3 However, the uneven distribution of white and grey matter may account for the exceptional abilities one can find in pupils with AS, such as calculating complex mathematical equations without the apparent need to process them, or a photographic memory by which large amounts of text can be quoted but with little comprehension. This is similar to someone knowing a shortcut and getting from A to B without really knowing how – it's just the way they have always done it.

   Faulty connections may also account for sensory issues. Super-efficient neural pathways may cause hypersensitivity and a flood of information so that the nervous system is constantly under pressure to process more than it can; and the lack of connectedness together with thin white matter and patchy grey matter can be the cause of hyposensitivity.

Trying to process tasks such as planning and writing an essay has been described to me as comparable to building a tower of cards – 'it's very hard!' An interruption by a well meaning TA or teacher sends the tower tumbling down. The person with an ASC cannot take up where they left off because of a poor working memory. How frustrating is that! You may see an angry child, because all the work they have constructed in their mind has gone and they have to start the whole process again from the very beginning.

The amygdala

The amygdala, a small part of the brain that, research has shown, has a major influence on much of the behaviour of a child on the spectrum, is responsible for recognizing and co-ordinating information from different parts of the brain and processing an emotional response. It is one of the areas in the brain responsible for recognizing social cues such as facial expressions and body language, in other words, the emotional responses of other people. In the early years the amygdala is enlarged in people with an ASC but shrinks to become smaller than normal in adolescence.

The amygdala triggers the flight or fight reflex. It is linked to the frontal cerebral cortex, which, depending on the information relayed, will suppress the reflex. For example, you see someone baring their teeth at you; your heart races, muscles tense, you feel hot and your hands sweat. These physical reactions are relayed to the hypothalamus, which regulates the emotion on a subconscious level in nanoseconds.

At the same time, the cerebral cortex and hippocampus evaluate the information, based upon knowledge or memories of similar past experiences, to make a judgement as whether or not there is a threat present. This information is relayed back to the amygdala through two inhibitory neurotransmitters called serotonin and glycine. In other words, the rational frontal lobe system overrides the basic instinct of the amygdala. If your brain reasons that someone is actually threatening you, you acknowledge that you are frightened and in danger and run in the opposite direction. If you recognize that he is smiling, your brain suppresses the desire to run away and you reach out to shake his hand in greeting.

The 'faulty wiring' in the brain connecting the amygdala to the frontal lobe, where impulses are controlled, may lead to a breakdown in communication. The individual with an ASC may be unaware of what is really happening. For example, when we get a fright after hearing a loud, unexpected noise and feel the adrenalin surge causing our heart to race and making us alert to everything around us, we are experiencing the same feeling as an individual on the spectrum. The difference is that in a nanosecond we assess the danger and quickly realize that it's actually not going to hurt us. There is nothing to be alarmed about, our heart rate returns to normal and we breathe a sigh of relief and calm down quickly. For the individual on the spectrum, the difficulties in processing what has happened mean that, instead of calming down, the panic rises as they try to work out what has happened. They want to understand, they can't, they become frustrated and angry and this feeling can last minutes, or hours, or the whole day.

Another aspect of the high levels of fear that the child feels is that their memories of that event will trigger the same reaction in the future when they are placed in a similar situation or with the same group of people. All those intense emotions will come pouring back and send them into a blind panic. Try to imagine what it must be like trying to function while experiencing such an onslaught on the senses and emotions.

It is important to understand that the neurobiological differences make a great impact on the behaviour of the individual with AS. It is not a choice, and it should inform the way we manage the pupil in school.

Can you imagine what it is like to be frightened every day of your life because your brain cannot predict what is going to happen next? Can you imagine trying to concentrate while your body is being tortured? Can you imagine living in a world surrounded by beings you cannot understand, where it feels like you have come from a different planet?

Further reading

Attwood, T. (2006). *The Complete Guide to Asperger Syndrome*. London: Jessica Kingsley Publishers.
Frith, U. (2003). *Autism, Explaining the Enigma*. 2nd edition, Oxford: Wiley-Blackwell.
*Jackson, L. (2003). *Freaks, Geeks and Asperger Syndrome*. London: Jessica Kingsley Publishers.

Website: http://www.autism.org.uk/about-autism/autism-and-asperger-syndrome-an-introduction.aspx
National Autistic Society (national charity), information, strategies and links to other useful sites.

3   Autism Spectrum Conditions in history

No-one really knows what causes autism. It is not a modern phenomenon. There are the old tales of changeling children who are stolen by the fairies and replaced with an identical child who screams and behaves 'badly'.

In her book, *Autism, Explaining the Enigma*, Uta Frith recounts a number of stories of people who display autistic behaviour.

Brother Juniper, who lived in Italy in the twelfth century, went to visit a sick brother in the hospital. When asked if there was anything he could do for him, the sick brother told Brother Juniper he'd love to have a pig's foot to eat. Brother Juniper went into the forest with a knife from the kitchens and cut off the foot of a live pig and carefully prepared a meal, which the sick brother enjoyed enormously. The owner of the maimed pig complained to the Franciscans but Brother Juniper could not comprehend what he had done wrong.

He was also in the habit of giving people anything they asked for, including his clothes. After this happened a few times, he was told not to do it any more, so the next time he was asked for clothing Brother Juniper told the beggar that he could not give him his habit but if the beggar took it off him he would not stop him.

Frith also describes the Holy or Blessed Fools of Russia, who she believes may have been autistic. They had no social awareness. Some roamed around naked, having a lack of sensitivity to pain, cold or hunger. They are reported as exhibiting bizarre, ritualistic behaviour: Pelagija Serebrenikova, for example, collected stones and bricks and placed them beside a flooded pit. She threw them all into the water. Then, when all the stones and bricks had gone; she waded into the pit and threw them out onto dry land; she then waded out of the pit and threw them back into the water again. She repeated this ritual for years.

Some of these holy fools were mute; others ranted in the streets and talked gibberish, parroted people or spoke inappropriately. Treated with tolerance because of their isolation and physical hardship, they were considered touched by God and their bizarre behaviour given significance in legends as lessons in life. They addressed Tsars and religious leaders without fear. Blessed Basil, fool for Christ, who robbed from the rich to feed the poor, is probably the most famous holy fool. He was canonized despite his criticism of Ivan the Terrible, who he confronted about his brutality.

Today the most famous people with autism are Dr Temple Grandin, Professor of animal science, inventor, author and lecturer in autism education; Stephen Wiltshire, artist; and Carly Fleischmann, author and non-verbal autistic, who in 2013 at the age of 18 started her degree at the University of Toronto.

4   A brief history of Asperger Syndrome

Asperger Syndrome is different from classic autism and is the most common form of autism found in mainstream schools. It is named after Hans Asperger (pronounced with a hard g), an Austrian psychiatrist, who wrote a paper in 1944 about his observations of a group of children. While of average or high intelligence, they displayed untypical behaviour: they used formal and unconventional language; had poor social skills; lacked empathy for their peers; had an all-absorbing interest that dominated conversation; displayed idiosyncratic behaviour; and were physically awkward. Lorna Wing, a British psychiatrist, coined the name in 1981, in a paper in which she described Asperger's symptoms in a group of children she was studying.

In 1989 Christopher Gillberg, Professor of Child and Adolescent Psychiatry at Gothenburg University, Sweden, published the first set of criteria for Asperger Syndrome. It is considered to be the closest to Asperger's original description of the condition.

Little was known about Asperger's work in the English-speaking world until 1991, when Professor Uta Frith, a psychologist, translated his paper from German into English.

In 1992 Asperger Syndrome was included in the World Health Organization's *International Classification of Diseases* (ICD-10) and in 1994 it was added to the *Diagnostic and Statistical Manual of Mental Disorders* (DSM-IV), the American Psychiatric Association's (APA) diagnostic reference book. The criteria set out in these two publications are the most popular reference for a diagnosis.

However, Asperger Syndrome as a separate condition has been removed from the APA's fifth edition of the *Diagnostic and Statistical Manual of Mental Disorders* (DSM-V), published in May 2013. It has been replaced by the umbrella term Autistic Spectrum Disorder, with three levels of severity, in order to provide a more precise diagnosis. However, recent fMRI (brain scan) research suggests that Asperger Syndrome is measurably different from autism.

It is generally agreed that Asperger Syndrome is genetic, although brain damage caused by accidents, for example, can result in the person developing autistic characteristics. The greater prevalence of AS today can be explained by better diagnosis, larger populations and higher survival rate among children. I also believe that the environment we live in today is not very autism friendly and the difficulties of AS children are more obvious. Education is a social activity: we expect children to work in pairs or groups, to discuss ideas and share opinions. A person with AS has social difficulties rooted in language impairment and rigid behaviour and will, therefore, stand out more in the modern classroom. Children with AS have fewer problems with speaking, although they can be quite literal in their interpretation of language, and are often of average, or above average, intelligence.

Autism spectrum conditions cannot be 'cured' with medical intervention, although there are a number of therapies that may lessen the effects of the condition. It is a disorder of the brain, not a mental illness, although other illnesses such as depression, learning disorders such as dyslexia, and motor difficulties such as hypermobility and dyspraxia may also co-exist.

Famous people diagnosed with Asperger Syndrome today include the actor Paddy Considine; singer songwriter Pip Brown, aka Ladyhawke; Gary McKinnon, computer hacker; and Clay Marzo the professional surfer.

5   Girls with Asperger Syndrome

According to statistics, only 1 in 4 people diagnosed with AS are female. There is growing concern that girls are being overlooked and that the figure is nearer 1 in 2. Females with AS seem to be better able to mask the condition by observing and copying their peers and therefore appear to be more socially adept. However, you will often find that they have few friends and tend to focus on one person at a time.

Girls have better imaginations than boys and often have a 'fantasy' life and invisible friends. They may cloak their interests in typical female behaviour but they are more intensely involved or appear to be unconventional. They may be totally uninterested in their appearance and may even prefer to dress like a tomboy, or they are very interested in fashion and develop their own unique style. Others may imitate a peer in their appearance, which can be a difficult issue as they are unlikely to understand that this will upset the girl they have copied. Most girls with AS choose not to draw attention to themselves; they have learned that this world doesn't operate the way they see it, so they fall silent and observe. Girls with AS are extremely vulnerable and may form inappropriate attachments. These need to be observed carefully to ensure that they are not being abused.

Currently, the female pupil diagnosed with AS may appear to be more extreme because she fits into the male model of an individual with AS. It has now been recognized that many females with AS do not fit into the diagnostic criteria of AS, which is heavily biased towards the behaviour of boys. There is a movement to develop a range of criteria in the future appropriate to the diagnosis of girls with AS.

There is a critical need in this area, not least to address the mental health issues associated with women on the spectrum, particularly among those who are not yet diagnosed. A growing body of autobiographical literature written by women who were diagnosed later in life reveal that many suffer from depression, anxiety, eating disorders, self-harm, behavioural problems and show a lack of social skills especially in group situations, while able to sustain a close friendship with one other person at a time, and this person may change frequently.

Further reading

Riley-Hall, E. (2012). *Parenting Girls on the Autism Spectrum: Overcoming the Challenges and Celebrating the Gifts*. London: Jessica Kingsley Publishers.
*Sainsbury, C. (2003). *Martian in the Playground*. Sage Publications Inc.
*Simone, R. (2010). *Aspergirls, Empowering Females with Asperger Syndrome*. London: Jessica Kingsley Publishers.

Website: http://taniaannmarshall.wordpress.com

6 Parents are a valuable resource – use them

The mother knows the child better than anyone else. If the child is seven years old, that is the amount of time it takes to be awarded a PhD, so a mother of a seven-year-old child has an honorary PhD in the study of that child. I know to listen to mother's knowledge and advice. She will provide continuity and experience for the child's lifetime.

Tony Attwood

Writing this chapter as a parent of a child with Asperger Syndrome, I would like to say that we really appreciate professionals who take the time to talk to us and learn about AS in order to inform themselves about the best way to support our children.

With all the challenges that face our children and the lack of understanding of autism in mainstream education, we have high levels of anxiety too. All we ask is that you remember Every Child Matters and our children need you to understand what it means to have autism and how that impacts on their daily lives. Also consider how having a child on the spectrum affects our daily lives too, as we organize our days to support our children, helping them to feel safe and competent; wanting them to be valued and accepted for who they are. They are just children. Please, work with us to help our children. Below is a letter I have written on behalf of parents seeking to help support their children.

Dear SENCo,

I would like to offer you the opportunity to engage with me regarding (my child), who has been diagnosed with an Autism Spectrum Condition (ASC). Autism is a heterogeneous condition and I am uniquely placed to offer you information pertinent to (my child) and how we might best enable him/her to thrive under your care and fulfil his/her academic potential.

Having a diagnosis of an ASC means that (my child) has a lifelong, pervasive developmental disorder that affects the physiology of the brain, resulting in cognitive processing difficulties and impairments in language, sensory processing and social communication. My child has certain rigid behaviours, a need for routine and is hyper or hypo sensitive to certain sensory input. His/her behaviour is not a choice but a direct result of different wiring in the brain.

As a hidden disability, autism means that (my child) may appear, on the surface, to be high functioning when, in reality, surviving the school environment, decoding instructions, meeting the education demands and negotiating social interactions in myriad situations requires a huge effort. This places huge stresses upon (my child) as s/he attempts to meet the expectations of teachers, teaching assistants and peers in circumstances that are often confusing due to a lack of understanding of what s/he is supposed to do. This can result in overload or burn out leading to shutdown or meltdown, which is distressing for all concerned.

I can be a valuable resource and help you to understand the impact autism has upon my child and suggest effective strategies to support him/her in your school. I would like to meet with you as soon as possible to discuss assessment of his/her needs and put together a range of strategies for the mutual benefit of (my child) and the school.

Sincerely…

A word in your ear

Delving into the histories of autistic families reveals clear evidence to suggest that AS is genetic. A family with a child with AS means that there is a high probability one or both parents are on the spectrum too. This should inform your dealings with them. Far too often we make judgements about mothers of children with AS who are struggling to get the best support for their child:

> The mum with Executive Functioning difficulties that forgets appointments (seen as neglect), the mum with Aspergers who struggles with tone in voice patterns (perceived as aggressive), the mum with Sensory Processing Disorder, who is in pain from sensory stimuli and is pacing (seen as a threat).
>
> Monique Blakemore

I know from my own experience, as both a TA and a parent, that we are considered to be quite difficult to deal with. As parents, all we want is to know that you are keeping our children safe, meeting their needs and enabling them to progress by building on their strengths.

Regular meetings (at least twice a term) with parents whose children are on the autism spectrum, regardless of whether they have a statement of SEN, are important and can be mutually beneficial. Work done in school may be supplemented at home in ways that are more appropriate to the child but which the school cannot provide, for example a trip to museums or even video games on the subject.

Introducing parents with Asperkids to each other can often lead to friendships outside school for the whole family. The pupils benefit by having more opportunities to develop their social skills and form meaningful relationships with their peers. The parents get support from other adults who understand better than anyone else what they are going through.

The comms book

A comms book is simply an exercise book in which TAs, teachers and parents relay information about how the pupils are managing their day in school and at home during term time. For example, a parent or carer may wish to communicate that the pupil has had a difficult start to the morning, having had a meltdown due to a row with a sibling, or the teacher tells the parents that their child worked particularly well in a lesson in a group, or the TA share that the pupil managed to cope with the fire alarm going off.

The book should be passed to the TA or teacher working with the pupil at the beginning of each lesson. It should be read by the teacher or TA in the next lesson because they will gain useful information about how the pupil is managing their day, how they are likely to perform in their lesson, and whether further adjustments need to be made.

Use the comms book to relay the following information:

- Progress in class: do not underestimate the value of praise, but it must be earned or the pupil will not trust you in future.
- Difficulties in lessons/subjects.
- Interaction with peers.
- Information about forthcoming changes to routines or staff, so that parents can prepare the pupil beforehand.
- School trips, activities, clubs and after school events; the pupil is unlikely to remember to pass on any notices of events to parents – staple these into the comms book!
- Questions of the other party if clarification is needed.
- Comments on health.
- Likes or dislikes.

The comms book can be used to apply consistency of approach across the curriculum during the school day, as school staff and parents share with each other what works effectively to support the pupil, help them to feel secure and keep them calm.

Families with a child with AS have higher levels of stress and anxiety than those with children with other special educational needs and are more likely to require support. Using a comms book to let them know how their child has managed the day will go a long way to reassure them that you are looking after their vulnerable child and monitoring any changes in behaviour. The pupil is unlikely to disclose what happened during the school day to their parents or carers until days, months or years after the actual event due to the way the autistic brain processes information.

Be honest! We can best support our children in mainstream education if you tell us the truth.

However, the comms book is *not* a *complaints* book. Always try and find something positive to say – negative comments are not seen as constructive criticism by pupils with AS and can have a devastating effect on self-esteem, so take care how you express anything negative. If they have access to the comms book and read it, they may take it personally and believe that you don't like them, and this will make supporting the pupil difficult. The best course is to suggest an alternative way of managing the situation: for example, Tom had difficulty queuing for his lunch today and pushed another pupil out of the way. He should be encouraged to show his pass and say 'excuse me' to the pupils he is overtaking.

Part Two

7 Be prepared! Transition into secondary school

Comparatively speaking, preparing to receive a pupil with AS into a secondary school is fairly easy. There is an abundance of information out there. Practical preparation for transition should take place at the very latest in the summer term before September entry. This is vital for the pupil with AS who may struggle to make sense of the world they live in: it is a very frightening place. The unexpected is terrifying and the source of great anxiety and stress. A change in routine and feeling of helplessness, not being able to control what is happening, might cause meltdown. Imagine this:

> You are in a city, in a foreign country, where you do not speak the language very well. You only understand bits of what is being said and can't really make any sense of it all. You keep making embarrassing social blunders because you don't know the social customs. The smells are overwhelming and the noise is giving you a headache. You're sweating buckets and feel physically uncomfortable in your own clothes. You don't know where to go; you keep getting lost; other people push you around and you're too scared to ask for help. You feel dizzy; you want to be sick. The food is disgusting. You are worried you are going to be late for your meeting; you don't know who is going to meet you or what is expected of you. They will probably talk at you for hours in a foreign language and you have to use an interpreter, who speaks with an accent you can't tune into. You will miss most of what they say and never be able to remember it and you've got to hold on until the end of the day when you can go back to your room. You need a quiet place; you want to be alone.

Children with AS are resistant to change because they are anxious and scared of the unknown: they want to do well but don't know what is expected of them. They cannot predict what's going to happen next and they may lack cognitive empathy and have difficulty imagining what you are thinking. Because you are in the same space at the same time, sharing the same experiences, they imagine that you are thinking exactly the same things as they are.

They get it wrong so often that the prospect of a new school, which is twice the size of their junior school, with twice as many pupils and 20 different teachers and TAs, is utterly petrifying. And not just for a few seconds or minutes – anxiety can persist for the whole of the school day.

To help prepare for September, learn as much as you can about each individual child with an ASC. They are all different and their condition will affect them in different ways.

The SENCo should assign at least two TAs to the pupil, so that if one is off there will be some continuity of care with the other TA, who is familiar to the pupil.

Strategies

Do your research

- Consult the parents or carers – they know their child better than anyone.
- Send the Transition Questionnaire to the primary SENCo and TAs, who will work with the prospective pupil, for them to complete, or visit the school yourself.
- Read the reports from the medical professionals involved in their diagnosis: psychologist, speech and language therapist, occupational therapist, physiotherapist, counsellors, everyone, and build up a positive profile.
- Use the Transition Questionnaire to record all the relevant information from all your sources.

Pupil Passport

Create a profile of the pupil for every member of staff who will be in contact with them on a regular basis, include ancillary staff: receptionists, administration staff, dinner ladies, librarians, technicians, caretaker and groundsmen.

- Include academic and social strengths, weaknesses, triggers and calming strategies.
- Add an 'Alert' if there are any issues that may put the pupil or others at risk, such as pica (eating non-edible material such as clothing or paint. In autism it is often associated with a sensory feedback and the child may wish to explore the item with their mouth, tongue and taste), or a phobia that causes an extreme reaction.
- Obtain a photograph of the pupil for the passport and a presentation to staff on Inset Day at the beginning of term (see below).
- Give the passport to staff and have a master copy in a file in the staffroom for cover supervisors, supply teachers and other visitors who come to work with the pupil's class.

School visits

Invite the prospective pupil to visit the school, several times if necessary.

- If you are going to be the pupil's key TA, you should accompany the child on all their visits.
- Assign an old pupil from the same primary school the year above the child to accompany them. (Check with the primary school that your choice is suitable. The old pupil may have forgotten teasing the child in the past but the child with AS will not.)
- Give the prospective pupil a map of the school with subject areas colour coded or identified with symbols. Ensure that a haven is clearly marked and take them there first; this may be the AS unit or Learning Support Centre, where the prospective pupil can feel safe, with sympathetic staff who understand their difficulties and how he or she may be supported.
- Have them bring a camera to record the visit. Take photographs of the pupil in places that interest them. This will help them to visualize themselves in these new surroundings. When they return to their primary school they can then make a booklet and familiarize themselves with their new school during the summer holidays.
- The pupil should also take photographs of key staff: the Principal, admin staff, receptionists, dinner ladies, school caretaker, librarian, head of year, SENCo, TAs, and form tutor if known.

Taster lessons

Invite the pupil to attend lessons in their favourite subject.

- They could join the pupil from their school who originally accompanied them for these taster sessions, together with the TA and accompanying primary TA.
- Use this as an opportunity to observe and record how the pupil with AS reacts in lessons with support from their primary TA.
- On another visit to the secondary school you could work with the pupil and begin to build a good working relationship.
- One visit should also cover break or lunchtime, to have them in the Base or Learning Resource and meet the other pupils.
- This is also an opportunity to observe their social skills.

Welcome Pack

This could be sent to the prospective pupil and include:

- A timetable either colour coded or with subject symbols.
- Days for assemblies.
- School rules.
- 'Unwritten' rules that may be overlooked. Briefly outline expected standards of behaviour.
- What to do if bullied, property is lost, homework diary goes missing and homework is not completed.
- Uniform and PE kit – photographs.
- A First Day in School Programme of Events – this will help prepare the pupils for a special assembly or any deviation from the normal timetable.

Inset Day presentation

- SENCo should introduce the whole staff to the pupils with AS.
- The presentation should include a photo of the pupils with a run-through of their AS passport.
- All staff should take note. They may not teach them but they may encounter the pupils elsewhere. Knowing he or she has AS may make a world of difference to the way they handle a situation, and to that pupil.

First day at school in September

- Meet the pupil as you did during the visits to the school in the summer term. The same experience will help to settle them.
- The key TA, who escorted the pupil during the summer term visits, should be assigned to work with the pupil for the first week at the very least.
- Have a written plan of the day ready to go over with them so that they know what to expect. Remember to include a map of the school.
- Make sure they know how to get from the form room to the haven and that it is also clearly marked on the map.

Build a relationship based upon understanding and respect

Lastly, and probably most importantly, sit down and talk to the pupil regularly, get to know them. This will help you build a relationship of trust and find out what they don't like which is likely to cause stress. Find out what they do like and what may calm them down.

- This information will help you to develop bespoke strategies and options to enable them to help themselves: exit cards, mood meter, haven – they may prefer the library or the gym and weight machines.

Top Tip

Involve everyone in the school in autism awareness. Anywhere, at any time, the pupil may need the help of a person who understands what they are going through. Being prepared to deal with a situation will make them feel 'accepted, safe, valued and competent' (Bill Nason).

Transition Questionnaire

Name:	
Primary School:	
Date:	
Additional Learning Difficulties	
Communication with home, regular meetings, communications book, telephone, email, recording device…?	
Sensory Issues?	
Other causes of distress: teasing, criticism, reprimanding…	
Tell Signs of Distress	
Alert System – Smileys, 5 point scale, traffic lights	
Calming Strategies, Stims	
Use of Social Stories or Comic Conversations in school or at home	
Special Interests	
Timetable – visual, colour coded, written	
Movement between lessons, locker, bag, TA, tray in SEN Base	
Communication	
Learning Style – visual, aural, kinaesthetic	
Concentration Level	
Strengths	
Weaknesses	
Flexibility	
Social Skills	

The Pupil Passport

The Pupil Passport should be available to all staff before the pupil arrives.

Putting a poster with photographs of all pupils with an ASC in the staffroom will help staff who don't teach them to recognize them around the school and in the playground. If there is a problem with the pupil's anti-social behaviour the teacher will know that this is more likely to be a result of his/her ASC rather than any malicious intent. Or if the pupil is on the periphery of other pupils messing around and s/he reacts badly to being shouted at, it will be invaluable to the member of staff on duty to know why.

Print the Pupil Passport on brightly coloured paper and distribute it to key staff: his/her teachers, support staff, senior management team, on call team, cover supervisors, and supply teachers as necessary. The Pupil Passport should be treated as confidential information.

Keep the writing to a minimum: use key words. All school staff need to be able to access the information quickly, in some cases just before the start of a lesson.

Include the following information:

- Name, form, form tutor and a passport size photograph
- Strengths
- Top Tips
- Stress inducers
- Calming strategies
- Alert: for any self-harming behaviour or pica (eating non-edible material).

To support a pupil with AS in having a smooth transition from primary to secondary school, including downloadable templates for Pupil Passports, go to the web link below; No. 12 on page 19 has a range of resources you can use.

Use the list below to gather all the relevant information for your passport. On the final page bullet point all the points you need to draw their attention to:

- **Strengths:** grammar, punctuation, long term memory.
- **Support strategies:** sit by door, diagrams, organization and planning using templates, consistency.
- **Triggers or stressors:** shouting, lights, teasing.
- **Calming strategies:** Stim – stroking velvet in pocket, time out, carrying heavy books.
- **Alert:** Phobia – spiders, wasps.

Top Tip

The Autism Education Trust has lots of resources for teachers and TAs.

Website

http://www.aettraininghubs.org.uk/wp-content/uploads/2012/06/AET-National-Autism-Standards_distributed.pdf

Affix
'passport' photo
here

Name:..

Form:..

Tutor:..

Room:..

My Strengths: ....

....

....

Support Strategies: ....

....

....

....

....

Triggers or Stressors: ....

....

....

Calming Strategies: ....

....

....

....

Name of Key Staff: ....

8 Sensory overload: strategies for creating an autism-friendly environment

People with ASCs perceive the world and relate to it very differently from NTs, and this makes them act differently too. One of the reasons for this altered perspective is that the brain is wired in a way that makes them hypersensitive or hyposensitive to aspects of their environment, probably as a result of over-connectivity or under-connectivity. Sensory overload is often the key to negative emotional and behavioural responses due to stress and fear.

> The sensory overload caused by bright lights, fluorescent lights, colours and patterns makes the body react as if being attacked or bombarded, resulting in such physical symptoms as headaches, anxiety, panic attacks or aggression.
>
> Donna Williams

If a pupil with an ASC gets upset for no apparent reason, look carefully at how they are reacting to their environment. Is there a sensory reason for the behaviour?

A typical day in school for the pupil with hypersensory interaction with the environment:

Registration – clothes itchy, people milling around, talking, laughing, screaming, bells! Leave me alone – be quiet. This chair is uncomfortable.

Corridors – crowded, noisy, out of control. Why did you hit me? Where am I going? No one told me we were in a different room today. Why are we doing history in a geography room? Where is my history teacher? Who are you? You stink of coffee. I feel sick.

Lessons – bright lights humming. I've got a headache. What does she expect me to do? Her voice hurts. I don't understand. Why doesn't she tell us to do one thing at a time instead of ten? I can't listen and write at the same time. She talks too fast. He's talking Japanese. What did he say? I've forgotten what to do. But she said to do that. Oh, it was Don't do that!

What does she want me to copy from the board? There's a red mark in the bottom corner of the board. There's too much stuff. Where is the bit I need to copy? I can't see it. The writing looks funny. He's spelt that word wrong. I wasn't being rude – you've made a mistake. I'm not copying a mistake.

What's the tune they're playing in the music room? Someone's coming up the stairs. Why is she shouting at me? I haven't done anything wrong!

What's that disgusting smell? I feel sick. This feels revolting – yeuch.

TA: *'Sam, where are you on a scale of 1–10? 8! Okay, let's get out of here!'*

When you see the pupil drop his or her head, put their hands over their ears, hug themselves, flap, pull their jumpers over their heads, make a strange noise or scream and run away, remember that hypersensitivity to certain things can make them simply too much to bear for the child and they can shut down or melt down.

The seven sensory systems affected by autistic processing difficulties are: hearing, sight, touch, taste, smell, balance (vestibular) and space and movement (proprioception). Sensory stimuli disturbances are varied and particular to the individual. By making small adjustments to the pupil's environment and allowances for the pupil's hypersensitivities, you will enhance their ability to learn by dampening the physical impact of sensory overload, thereby reducing anxiety and fear.

Similarly, if you judge the pupil is behaving in a certain way because they crave sensory input, giving them the appropriate stimulation (also called sensory snacks) during the school day to stabilize their senses will enable them to concentrate better during lessons.

When senses are disorganized, the ability to pay attention, learn and communicate are negatively affected and it may be helpful at this point to take time out.

Time out

Time out is a strategy that should be agreed before being put into use. It is not removal from the lesson as a punishment. Discuss the following with the pupil beforehand:

- Time out is to support the pupil in times of sensory overload and distress.
- The Bombmeter (see page 42) is a tool to help you to gauge their stress level. Remove at 8+. As you get to know your target pupils you may be able to distract them and talk them down, but in the meantime take time out at 8+.
- The pupil is to go to the agreed place – library, haven, reception – before going for a walk outside.
- Agree a time limit (be flexible) with the pupil beforehand; 10–15 minutes, then return to class to resume work.
- Any work missed should be caught up in pupil's free time such as break or lunch; be sensitive and flexible.

Stimming

Stimming is a form of self-regulation of the senses and results in self-stimulatory behaviour. Stim (verb) is short for 'indulging in self-stimulatory behaviours' or (noun) a 'stimulatory behaviour'. Pupils on the autism spectrum stim to distract themselves from something that is upsetting them, in an attempt to calm down. A stim is used to stimulate one sense in an effort to block out distractions from another sense in order to self-calm when distressed or anxious. People with an ASC also stim when they are happy or excited.

Stimming comes in many forms and is usually a repetitive movement of the body like rocking, tapping, bouncing, flapping of arms or hands, swaying from side to side and fiddling with or stroking an object. A pupil may stroke a piece of velvet, fiddle with a piece of string or squeeze a rubber ball to distract themselves from flickering lights or the sound of electricity buzzing through the wall.

Other stims include funny noises, facial expressions, singing, humming, talking or babbling to oneself, clearing one's throat, nail (and finger) biting. Many of these behaviours are not tolerated socially in school, so a lot of work is done at home or in primary school to establish a more acceptable alternative using a sensory toy – a squeeze ball or everyday object such as a piece of string – which the pupil finds soothing.

NTs stim too: tapping their pens or feet and drumming fingers! What's your stim? It is an unconscious act. We don't stim to annoy people. It might be annoying, but used as a calming tool it should be allowed to continue until a more acceptable or discreet alternative is found to replace the behaviour. Stimming enables the pupil to concentrate on their work.

If you insist that the pupil stops stimming you will undermine their ability to do a task. They will have to use more of their reduced or depleted executive functioning skills to regulate their unconscious behaviour and, therefore, reduce their ability to perform well in the task set.

Difficulties with the seven senses

Sound

Auditory disturbance is a common sensory issue for individuals with AS. They can often hear things we can't: the buzzing of lights, electricity, road noise and voices in another room are all distracting. Noise levels or pitch may be painful, including a certain person's voice. Potential difficulties may be found in Music lessons with particular instruments; Technology with power tools and food mixers; the acoustics of the gym or main hall in PE or Dance; and the sound of a vacuum cleaner.

An acute sense of hearing means that the pupil can hear what is going on in the next room but cannot make sense of what the person sitting next to them is saying. Oversensitivity to certain sounds – crisp packets scrunching, someone eating meringues – is like the sound of nails on a chalkboard to a NT, and humming lights sound like a swarm of bees.

There may also be difficulties with processing long-winded, oral instructions because words become jumbled.

The pupil may also talk very loudly or quietly, in a monotonous voice. They may have little awareness of the volume of their own voice.

Strategies

- Ear defenders are very effective but a discreet earplug is more desirable.
- Give short, clear oral instructions.
- Check that those instructions have been heard and understood by asking 'What did Mr Bennett tell you to do?'
- Write down instructions and support comprehension with symbols or images.
- If the pupil shows signs of distress due to noise levels, remove them from the classroom to a quiet area until they are calm.
- Warn them beforehand when the bells or fire alarms are about to go off and take appropriate action.
- Alert the pupil through discreet signals if he or she is talking loudly.
- Make them aware of the volume by recording a conversation to indicate the two levels – shouting and normal range.

Sight

Visual disturbance may be caused by bright or flickering lights, which we don't see. Individuals with AS have also reported their vision as being similar to over-exposure in a photograph, and colours appearing to be brighter than on the typical spectrum. The object they are looking at may appear distorted or even moving about. They may also be sensitive to a particular colour.

Some pupils are distracted by displays of work on the wall or a cluttered desk and are therefore unable to concentrate on the task.

Detailed focus processing is both a strength and weakness. Pupils may be unable to see the whole because they are captured by the detail. However, an attention to detail can be an advantage in certain tasks, provided they are not compelled to strive for perfection and destroy something that they perceive as sub-standard.

When reading text to pupils on the autism spectrum they may have difficulty tracking lines of writing across paper. Hand to eye co-ordination may be clumsy because there are problems with depth perception (see also Movement – Proprioception, below).

In times of stress, blurring may occur on the periphery of their vision or in the centre of their focus. Images may fracture and faces become distorted like Picasso's paintings.

Strategies

- Switch off some or all of the lights.
- Allow the pupils to wear tinted lenses or sunglasses indoors.
- Replace the colour of background in a display or have it out of the line of sight of the pupil.
- Seat the pupil in a visually calm zone of the classroom facing a bare wall, or use a portable desk carrel (a three-sided, hinged screen).
- Remove the displays around the board or where the teacher stands at the front of the class.
- Keep the work area clear and clutter free.
- Use reading blinds to cover irrelevant text, diagrams or pictures in textbooks.
- Write on the board in different colours for each sentence in rotation to help differentiate between one sentence and the next.
- Use gels to put over text.
- Photocopy text onto beige or grey rather than white paper.
- Use different colour inks to differentiate between subject matter, for example characters; geographical characteristics in different areas; opinion versus fact.
- Teach the pupil how to cross out errors neatly or use a pencil or a laptop.
- Be patient and allow time to process.
- The haven in the AS base or SEN base should be visually clear – avoid wall displays.

Touch

Tactile disturbance can result in a light touch causing the pupil pain because the nerves activated on the superficial level are disordered or hyper-sensory; whereas a firm hold is comforting. This may cause problems during transitions between lessons in a crowded corridor and accusations of being assaulted by others in the hustle.

Clothing may feel itchy or be painful to wear: wool feels like fibreglass, labels 'lacerate' the skin. Handling certain textures such as those found in Art, Science or Technology, like paint and cooking ingredients, may be intolerable. Water on the face can cause panic in swimming lessons.

Hyposensitivity is common in tactile sensory integration. Pupils with AS may be insensitive to temperature or pain, which may cause problems because extreme cold or heat can still do damage even if you don't feel it. An extraordinary high threshold of pain can mean that the pupil may break a bone and not realize it. It may lead to behaviour that seeks stimulation such as bumping into things or even self-harm.

Some individuals with AS relate to their environment through touch, feeling everything. Many use the sensation of certain textures, which others find repellent, to keep calm, and this should be modified if socially offensive.

> James, aged 15, was a boy with a horrible habit. He would blow his nose into a handkerchief and then work the phlegm between his fingers. It was pointed out to him that this was socially unacceptable but the comfort he derived from the experience overrode any social inhibitions or requests to desist. Eventually, with support from home, as well as in school, it was replaced by the contents of a slime jelly egg.

Blu-tack is often used as a tactile stim. You may find displays littered over the floor around the school and a pupil with a rather large, sticky, blue ball of tack in their pocket.

Strategies

- Allow the pupil to move between lessons a couple of minutes before everyone else or accompany them at a discreet distance, or beside them if they prefer.
- Plastic gloves can be useful or can cause more problems.
- Cut out labels from clothing and try and be flexible in allowing alternatives to irritating clothing – it can be painful.
- Desensitization to the feel of certain things over a period of time may be helpful, but never force it. As the pupils get older they may become desensitized naturally.
- **Do not remove stims.** They help the pupil to regulate senses and emotions – if offensive, be imaginative and find a substitute. Put sensory stims into a box with a hole cut in the front, which can be unblocked to allow discreet access to them.

Taste and smell

Gustatory and **Olfactory** disturbances can result in the pupil being a very picky eater with a very restricted diet. Food may be separated on a plate or on separate plates. Strongly flavoured food may become too tasty after a while and the rest of the meal be left on the plate. Any wrongness like chicken and bacon tasting of fish will be noticed!

Perfume or deodorants can be overpowering and stifling, making the pupil nauseous. They may complain about a smell of burning from electric wires heating up, which is imperceptible to typical senses. Or they may smell in order to seek extra information about an object, place or person, which can be a little off-putting if you don't understand why. Remember that their perception of the world is fragmentary. If they do smell overtly, you may be able to find a particular scent that the pupil will find calming.

> Melanie, aged 13, loves going to restaurants with her father. One of her favourite puddings is chocolate fudge cake. They share one between them. Melanie cannot finish it all because 'It's too tasty'. Her father never takes her to an Italian restaurant. Melanie cannot stand the texture of pasta.

Strategies

- Tolerance and flexibility are needed in the dining hall and Food Technology classes.
- When eating, let the pupils separate food out or they may be unable to eat it.
- In Food Technology, remember that a strong reaction to the smell and taste of food may be part of the way the condition impacts upon the pupil and find an alternative.
- If you are with a pupil who cannot stand the smell of perfume or deodorant, avoid wearing it that day.
- If you have a pupil with a favourite smell, which helps concentration and keeps them calm, use it under advice from parents. Aromatherapy strategies can be very soothing and enable the pupil to concentrate in examinations, for example, by blocking out other stimuli.

Balance

Vestibular system disturbance is where the inner ear receives misinformation from movement, speed and direction about where we are in space. Hypersensitivity in the vestibular system can result in feeling as though they are falling when standing up or sitting down – which can make them clingy when moving around; or a feeling of nausea similar to carsickness or seasickness. They have a fear of heights and going up or down stairs. There may be difficulties in sitting, or changing direction and speed, causing clumsiness. They are unlikely to ride a bike and will avoid anything that appears to be a bit risky.

If the pupil has a hyposensitive vestibular system they will be constantly on the move, seeking thrills and always running around; rocking the body and shaking the leg. The need for vestibular stimulation may show itself by the pupil spinning in the playground or swinging off branches, and rough play with peers.

Strategies

- Understanding, tolerance and patience.
- Time out of the PE or Dance lesson, to recover if nauseous.
- Vestibular stimulation exercises in PE or Dance, for example, hanging upside down, swinging from side to side, spinning, rolling, somersaulting, cartwheels and dancing.
- Time in the sensory room on a gently swinging hammock (side to side swing).

Movement

Proprioception system disturbance – the way the brain perceives the body in space and controls our limbs or the movement system may be disordered. Poor motor planning means that what we do automatically, like putting one foot in front of the other to walk, may need a conscious thought in order to complete the action. Poor motor control means not knowing how to get the brain to tell the body what to do. The child has to consciously think about their movements and this makes them slow and clumsy.

Jake, aged 11, pretends he doesn't see street lamps and walls as he walks down the road. He's always bumping into things accidentally on purpose and pretending to be Harold Lloyd or Buster Keaton. He also runs his hand along hedges or walls. He needs to be in touch with his environment to make sense of it as he moves through the space.

Some children with ASCs walk on their tiptoes. There are a number of theories for this, including sensory aversion to having the whole foot on the ground, but it has also been suggested that it is related to vestibular or visual disturbance. Whichever, it contributes to the problems with motor skills.

Having poor gross motor skills means that the pupil may walk with a strange gait, veer off line slightly and be unable to change direction without great effort. Lolling or leaning on a wall or even against another person may be the pupil just trying to rest. Navigating transitions between lessons through crowded corridors may be a challenge. There is often a lack of co-ordination, clumsiness and the use of inappropriate force; this makes playing team sports in PE difficult, for example kicking a ball too hard or too gently.

Difficulties with movement can also affect fine motor skills: holding a pen, a paintbrush or cooking utensils; manipulating small objects in Technology. Writing may be a struggle, the pencil may be pushed too hard and snap. A laptop is a useful tool, although typing can also be tricky, especially if the pupil has hypermobility in his fingers, a common trait in AS.

Strategies

- Understanding, tolerance and patience.
- Leave lessons 2 minutes early and accompany the pupil.
- Develop an individual programme of exercises for the pupil to follow in PE, building up to a game of basketball or tennis. The smaller the team the better.
- Swimming is a popular individual sport and effective exercise, if they don't mind water on their face.
- Proprioception exercises in PE, e.g. using weights, bouncing on a trampoline or pushing heavy objects.
- Gross motor skills exercises in PE, e.g. catching and throwing, kicking and dribbling.
- Fine motor skills exercises with chopsticks and dried peas, cross-stitch, putting pegs into holes, tying shoe laces.
- Use a laptop for written work.

Warning: Watch out for overstimulation! Too much spinning can lead to extreme motion sickness and the pupil may end up being unable to sit, stand or lie down without feeling nauseous. It is very similar to chronic car or seasickness and very unpleasant.

Summary

The pupil with AS may display a range of negative behaviours because of their sensory issues:

- Distraction and the inability to plan and organize or start or finish a task.
- Poor motor skills and clumsiness.
- Hyperactivity and over-reaction.
- Zoning out and withdrawing.
- Isolation and emotional confusion.
- Agitation and anxiety, frustration and anger.
- Inability to exert self-control.
- Tiring quickly.
- Self-stimulation or self-harm – flapping, hitting the body or head banging.

It is crucial to identify any sensory issues from the outset. Sensory disturbances may lead to overload, when their brains receive too much information and shut down. Noise levels are a common problem for people with AS. I have left classrooms on many occasions with highly distressed pupils to get them away from the noise. A lack of awareness of a particular sensitivity and a failure to act can quickly lead to a meltdown. In certain situations, behind the explosive outburst, the anger and frustration is, very likely, a child in pain.

Use the Sensory Integration Difficulties Checklist at the end of this section to ascertain whether your target pupil has any specific difficulties which may impact on their learning or social inclusion. You can fill in a copy from your observations and I would advise sending another copy home to be completed by the pupil's parents or carers.

A mainstream school must be absolute hell for children who have sensory integration problems on several levels. Their brains work harder to compensate for the difficulties they experience. Managing the daily assault on their senses means harnessing parts of the brain not usually associated with the function. At the end of the day, having held it all together at school, the child may be utterly exhausted or overstimulated and go into shutdown or meltdown at home, and the parents have to deal with the fallout.

This is one of the reasons why homework is so difficult for the pupil with AS. Apart from the fact that it is quite clearly schoolwork and should, logically, be done at school, they may be totally incapable of doing it.

While they are in school they rely on a key worker and ever-vigilant staff to help them. They need your understanding, tolerance and patience and above all to be kept safe.

Try to imagine what it must be like to go to an open air concert, where you are listening to loud music you don't particularly like, in the middle of a packed, pumped up, screaming crowd of people who haven't had a bath in 3 days, in a muddy field with lights flashing at you and being trapped there. Now imagine dealing with that for 7 hours a day, 5 days a week...

Further reading

Myles, B.S., Cook, K.T., Miller, N.E., Rinner, L. and Robbins, L.A. (2005 reprint). *Asperger Syndrome and Sensory Issues: Practical solutions for making sense of the world.* Autism Asperger Publishing Co.

Websites

A is for Autism, BBC Four: http://www.youtube.com/watch?v=cPR2H4Zd8bl
http://www.sensory-processing-disorder.com/
Sensory Overload Simulation – WeirdGirlCyndi http://www.youtube.com/watch?v=BPDTEuotHe0
A Child's View of Sensory Processing – ESGWNRM http://www.youtube.com/watch?v=D1G5ssZlVUw
http://musingsofanaspie.com/2013/06/18/a-cognitive-defense-of-stimming-or-why-quiet-hands-makes-math-harder/

Sensory Integration Difficulties Checklist

Pupil:.. Form:..

Age:.. Date:...

1. Auditory System – Sound	Often	Sometimes	Never
Hypersensitivity			
Distracted by imperceptible sounds – lights humming, electrical wires			
Distracted by background noises – chatter, cars, other class's noise			
Starts at unexpected sounds – sirens, shouting			
Frightened of certain sounds – vacuum cleaner, drill, hairdryer			
Puts hands defensively over ears in noisy environments – classroom, halls, cinema, sports events			
Reacts badly to a certain person's voice			
Asks people to be quiet			
Cannot concentrate in a noisy environment			
Becomes agitated and disruptive during noisy activities			
Avoids going to assemblies or participating in large group activities			
Tunes out of what's going on around them			
Relaxes in quiet environment, when spoken to quietly			
Hyposensitivity			
Does not respond to name being called			
Forgets oral instructions immediately			
Does not appear to understand what has been said			
Talks self through a task			
Cannot pinpoint origin of sound			
Cannot hear certain sounds			
Ignores some sounds			
Likes loud music or turns volume up on TV, iPod			
Makes a lot of noise			
Talks loudly			
Hums, coughs, clears throat			

Auditory Processing Difficulties			
Unable to filter out sounds and concentrate on speaker			
Asks speaker to repeat what has just been said			
Cannot fulfil more than one or two instructions at a time			
Does not appear to have understood what has been said			
Difficulty expressing self in words			
Begins a sentence but loses the thread of what is being said			
Interrupts other people in mid flow			
Mispronounces words after hearing them			
Seeks reassurance from listener while talking			

2. Visual System – Sight	Often	Sometimes	Never
Hypersensitivity			
Distressed by bright lights, wears sunglasses indoors			
Difficulty discerning shape/form in busy background			
Distracted by displays, pictures, clouds other visual stimuli			
Distressed by a certain colour or bright tones			
Rubs eyes after reading			
Cannot focus on text, reading and writing tasks			
Avoids eye contact			
Fixated by detail, stares intently at something			
Likes being in a dark room			
Hyposensitivity			
Loses place when reading or sequence work e.g. maths problems			
Misreads words, mispronunciation			
Reads words backwards – was = saw,			
Cannot see whole picture, focuses on details/patterns			
Complains about visual disturbance – seeing double, blurred vision			
Poor handwriting – different sized letters, writing along a line			
Poor hand–eye co-ordination when cutting out or drawing shapes			

3. Tactile System – Touch	Often	Sometimes	Never
Hypersensitive			
Reacts to a light touch as if it hurt, rubs the place touched			
Dislikes being touched, won't touch another person			
Stands apart from others, withdraws from when approached			
Rolls up sleeves, frequently adjusts clothes			
Intolerant of certain textures, wool, labels in clothing, socks, hats			
Dislikes having hair cut or brushed, nails clipped, teeth brushed			
Cannot tolerate messy play – paint, sand, dough, glue			
Walks on tiptoes			
Dislikes new shoes or walking barefoot on grass, sand			
Distressed by water on face when swimming or washing face			
Dislikes certain textures of food and refuses to eat them			
Oversensitive to heat or cold			
Hyposensitive			
Touches everything and everyone, rubs hands together			
Hands in pockets			
Sits on hands			
Unaware of minor cuts and abrasions, high tolerance of pain			
Doesn't feel the cold, refuses to wear a coat out			
Seeks rough textures and revels in messy play			
Rough when playing with other children or pets			
Unaware of bumping into others – just barges past people			
Unaware of being dirty or snotty			
Seeks textural stimulation – repeated stroking, of clothing or blanket, rubs body along walls			
May hit or pinch themselves repeatedly, scratches, rubs, hits, pulls hair, bangs head against wall			

4. Vestibular System – Balance	Often	Sometimes	Never
Hypersensitive			
Poor balance when moving, sits down often			
Dislikes playground activities on equipment			
Afraid of heights even small ones – kerb			
Clumsy – falls over often			
Seems cautious when moving around, holds onto wall, railings, other people			
Avoids making rapid changes of direction			
May complain of feeling sick during physical activities			
Has difficulty riding a bike			
Hyposensitive			
Hyperactive, paces up and down			
Loves spinning, swinging, bouncing			
Impulsive and seeks thrills			
Always runs, jumps and rushes ahead of everyone			
Moves when sitting – rocking, leg shaking, head wags			
Turns upside down on chair			
Craves rapid movement			
Enjoys rough rides – amusement parks, on bike			

5. Proprioceptive System – Movement	Often	Sometimes	Never
Lacks Awareness of Movement and Appropriate Force			
Written work is untidy			
May break pencil by pressing too hard			
Frequently tears the paper when rubbing out			
Often breaks things			
Hurts people unintentionally with force of grip			
Uses too much force for everyday activities – stamping, slamming, yanking, shoving			
Seeks Sensory Input			
Tight clothing			
Stamps feet			
Chews fingers, pencils, clothing			
Crashes into things deliberately			
Cracks knuckles frequently			
Rough play with other children – hitting, bumping, shoving			
Leans heavily on things or people			

Poor Co-ordination and Poor Muscle tone			
Weak grip			
Poor motor skills, fine and gross			
Tires easily			
Difficulty doing up buttons or zip			

6. Gustatory System – Taste	Often	Sometimes	Never
Hypersensitive			
Picky eater – sticks to same food day after day in lunchbox, same dish in restaurants			
Can discern change in ingredients or wrong flavours – fishy flavour in bacon or chicken			
Prefers bland foods			
Only able to eat so much food, e.g. chocolate – too tasty			
Dislikes toothpaste			
Eats only hot or cold food			
Hyposensitive			
Chews clothing, pencils and other inedible objects			
Likes heavily flavoured food – salt, pepper, chilli			
Puts non-edible objects into mouth, chews string, paper, clothing			

7. Olfactory System – Smell	Often	Sometimes	Never
Hypersensitive			
Smells odours which go unnoticed by others			
Offended/nauseated by bodily odours			
Perfume/deodorants may be irritating			
Refusal to go into science labs, tech rooms or houses because of smell			
Likes or dislikes someone because of the way they smell			
Hyposensitive			
Doesn't appear to notice foul odours			
Overtly sniffs things to smell them			

Further Comments ....

....

....

....

....

....

....

....

....

Signed .... Date ....

Relationship to pupil ....

Sensory breaks and a sensory room

It is worth repeating that while most pupils with an ASC appear to be able to manage the typical school day, a short conversation with parents may tell a different story. Many families report that they melt down in response to the stress of the school day when they get home. It's like living through a tornado, as the child seeks sensory stimulation they have been denied in school; or the child goes straight to their bedroom and 'hides under their bed' until they have restored themselves, and some sleep for several hours to recover from the assault on their fragile nervous system.

If you can manage the sensory environment for each pupil with an ASC you will reduce stress and anxiety and help them manage their emotions and behaviour. So if your school doesn't have a sensory room already, it would make a great project for the Technology department.

Useful tools to have in a sensory room are: lava or bubble lamps, coloured lights and glitter ball (replace any strip or neon lighting with conventional or daylight bulbs); mp3 player to play favourite music or sounds, such as running water or a storm, from the pupil's iPod or SEN resources – if loud music is needed, let them listen to it on their ipod; aromatherapy oils; a texture wall or tapestry with different textured materials, and cushions made from different materials, for example, velvet and space blanket material; a swing hammock; large cushions or beanbags to lie on or snuggle under; weighted blankets; stress balls to knead; padded mats for a space on the floor to roll around on; and a pop up tent. These are suggested to stimulate or calm all the senses. Ask your pupils with an ASC what they would like to see, touch, listen to, smell and do in the sensory room.

Another effective, calming tool is a fish tank with brightly coloured fish. This may also be used to support an interest.

Time out in the sensory room should be timetabled so that the pupil can reset his or her nervous system. Activities should be designed to meet the individual pupil's needs and drawn up in consultation with an occupational therapist (OT). Time out in general should be an agreed strategy with strict time limits.

The sensory room should not be a padded cell. Never ever use the room for punishment or lock the child in it: it is a refuge; a place to calm down, not an isolation unit, and to place a child in a room to calm down and lock the door is unlawful imprisonment. The child should never be forced to go into a sensory room, and they should be able to leave when they wish.

A member of staff should also be in the room guiding activities. However, there have been a number of safeguarding issues and the best way to monitor what goes on in the room in order to keep both pupils and staff safe is to install a discreet video monitoring system.

You can find some good ideas on the Internet for sensory rooms and equipment, and companies that design and create sensory rooms for schools. However, it would be best to ask the pupil and the parents what they need and what works best.

Top Tip

I played instrumental music unobtrusively in the classroom while the class were getting on with writing tasks. It had the effect of enhancing levels of concentration and reducing unnecessary chatter, and had a measurably calming effect. The whole class benefited and their levels of concentration and work rate went up. The music should be a single instrument, not a full orchestra, and played at low volume. You can affect the mood of the classroom with the tempo.

Sensory Snacks

Timetabling sensory snacks into the day will reduce stress levels. Sensory snacks should be tailored to the individual pupil's needs based on the feedback from the sensory checklist, with input from an occupational therapist. For other pupils, the opportunity to spend a few minutes away from the class in a calm environment may be all that's needed.

I have walked pupils around the sports fields; taken them to a quiet area to sit in silence for a while; explored the textures of a variety of materials; lifted weights in the gym; taken them to a sink to feel running water pass through their hands. Ask the pupils what they would like to do.

Sensory Snacks	
Calming Senses	Alerting Senses
Sounds: classical music, whale song, rhythm, heartbeat, water trickling over rocks, thunderstorm	Rousing music – heavy metal, playing a musical instrument, dance music
Silence, reading, drawing	Dancing, running from one end of the gym to the other
Slow moving lights, fire light, lava lamps, fish tank	Flashing lights
Rocking chair, hammock	Swinging – quickly, changing direction
Wear rucksack with heavy books	Wear rucksack with heavy books
Jobs about the school: clean boards, errands, washing up, sorting cupboards	Jumping – trampoline
Textures – bowl of rice, sand, water, different materials	Weights room, lie under heavy cushions or weighted blankets
Squeeze ball, fidget	Moving heavy furniture, pushing against the wall
Sit or lie in a dark tent	Rolling on the floor
Wrapped tightly	Climbing bars
Pet club	Gardening club

Sensory Box

Each pupil can have a personalized sensory box to use discreetly in lessons. Place a number of articles in a shoe or tissue box with a discreet entry through the top or side. It should contain things the pupil likes the feel/smell/taste/look of. You don't have to spend money on sensory toys but include day-to-day objects, which will help keep the pupil's senses ordered; for example textured cloth, strings of beads, sponges, small cuddly toys, wood blocks, blu-tack, a stress ball. Ask the pupil what they would like.

9   The real challenge: managing behaviour

I have always had a problem with the term Challenging Behaviour when used to describe the behaviour of a child with a neuro-physiological condition: it suggests that the child has a choice. It does not acknowledge the real difficulties the child has processing what is happening and being able to respond to it rationally. Sensory overload and extreme anxieties arising from the need to meet demands within the time given in a pressurized environment, such as at school, are the conditions under which pupils on the spectrum are trying to function and sometimes they just can't cope.

Amber, aged 12, couldn't find her homework when she got into her lesson. She looked in her bag but it was a mess. She threw the bag on the floor, narrowly missing her TA and flung herself across the table. The TA assigned to Amber moved away from her to the back of the classroom. Amber picked up her bag and tried to find her homework again as her peers handed in their worksheets to the teacher. She still couldn't find it and threw the books on the floor followed by the bag. Her TA picked up the books and put them on the desk. Amber kicked the desk and was reprimanded by the TA, who moved to the back of the classroom. Amber put her head in her arms and started crying loudly, kicking her foot against the legs of the table.

At this point, another TA decided to intervene. He picked up Amber's bag off the floor and gathered together her books. 'I have done it, sir', she said pathetically.

'I know you have. We just need to find it, don't we?' Sitting at her table, he piled the contents of the bag into a big pile and went through it all methodically, finding the homework in less than a minute. Amber beamed at him, picked up her homework and handed it in proudly.

The rest of the lesson passed off without incident.

Amber's problem was executive functioning – her bag was full of paper and books she didn't need that day. She couldn't manage the demand to hand in her homework because she couldn't find it immediately. Greater pressure was placed on her as her peers handed in their homework and she just couldn't find hers quickly enough.

At lunchtime we weeded out all the work she didn't need in her bag and put it into an envelope file marked Homework. I wrote a note in her comms book relating the incident. I asked for the old work to be removed and for the file to be used to help her keep her current homework in one place in her bag. Knowing where her homework was reduced the stress of trying to find it in her messy bag. She happily used this simple strategy, which was supported at home by her parents.

Amber's TA focused on her aggressive behaviour. She felt Amber's behaviour was bad and as a 'reactive, punishment consequence' she withdrew her support, raising Amber's stress levels even higher. She felt Amber should have been able to go through her bag and find her homework herself. Amber couldn't manage the situation and needed support. She wasn't having a tantrum, she made two attempts to help herself but it was simply beyond her. She was frustrated, stressed, embarrassed and angry at herself.

Remember, bad behaviour may be a direct result of not being able to manage the emotional responses to certain situations due to the poor connectivity in the brain and raised levels of chemicals.

Heading off a meltdown by distracting the pupil with a favourite activity or what may be perceived as a 'reward' goes against everything we are taught: if a pupil cannot regulate their behaviour, we see it as our duty to impose our own discipline. We may have several problems with the choice of strategy a pupil uses to try to calm themselves. It may be seen as oppositional or avoidance behaviour – a refusal to do as they are asked – or rewarding what we see as 'bad' behaviour.

In a crisis situation we have to make a decision based on the outcome. I believe when we are trying to prevent a meltdown we should use whatever means we can to effect a good outcome, not only for the pupil but for the whole class and oneself. In this instance, a good outcome is to avoid a meltdown. This may mean fidgets, an activity different from the rest of the class, something to chew on, a walk around the school, whatever does the job of helping the child calm down and regain self-control.

It is not a power struggle. We often make the mistake of thinking we have to control others to get them to do what we want. Rather, it is about enabling the pupil to make the right decision: that they want to do what you want, to co-operate and work towards the same goal. It is the pupil's sense of well-being that matters, their self-confidence and belief that they can do what is demanded of them. If they believe they can, they will attempt it and in all likelihood succeed.

If it is too difficult, they fear failure, become distressed, frustrated and angry; and their behaviour may become oppositional and defiant. This is the tipping point – the next action you make can result in calming the situation or escalating the problem, which will lead to confrontation and meltdown.

Strategies

Elvén (2010) recommends strategies that are very effective with pupils with AS (and other processing difficulties like ADHD) in stressful situations that may escalate into violent confrontation:

- Step back away from them – reduce the threat by giving them space to calm down.
- Walk away – do not engage in escalation of a situation; return when the pupil has calmed down.
- Avoid eye contact – stand to one side out of the pupil's line of vision.
- Stop and listen to what the pupil has to say. Do not argue with them.
- Do not command or threaten; treat them as an equal and suggest a solution with an offer of help to support them in making the right decision.
- Offer two good choices: Do you need time out for 10 or 15 minutes? Would you like to go to the library and read, or the gym and work out for 15 minutes?
- Remember your goal is to help them regain control, not be in control of them.

Top Tip

Do not shout at a pupil with AS. They might react by shouting right back at you, reflecting your behaviour.

Lead by example: if you want calm, be calm; if you want co-operation, listen and co-operate – negotiate a compromise.

Strategy

Think ahead. There are lots of situations that will present difficulties for the pupil on the autism spectrum. The following are examples of scenarios you might wish to prepare for:

- forgotten something – homework, pencil case, PE kit
- fire alarm goes off…
- substitute teacher
- change of room
- change to timetable
- bullying.

Use the following template to help the pupil work out 'What I do If…'
  Describe a possible scenario:

  If I forget my PE kit.

  This is a problem because if I have PE I won't be able to participate and Mr Jones puts people who forget their PE kit into detention.

  I can sort this out by:
  1 Going to reception, calling my mother and asking her to bring it in.
  2 Leaving my PE kit in my locker.
  3 Borrowing PE kit from Mr Smith.
  4 Doing the detention.
  5 Checking my timetable every evening.
  6 Putting everything I need for tomorrow in my bag.

I have not put numbers past 1 on the template because many pupils with ASC cannot deal with lots of choices; some need to be told exactly what to do.
  Once the pupil or you have decided what is best for them to do, put it on a key fob so they can refer to it. This will help if it is a recurring difficulty.

Further reading

Elvén, B. H. (2010). *No Fighting, No Biting, No Screaming. How to make behaving positively possible for people with autism and other developmental disabilities.* London: Jessica Kingsley Publishers.

Template 9.1

What I can do

If_____

_____

_____

This is a problem because _____

_____

_____

_____

I can sort this out by:

1. _____

_____

_____

_____

_____

_____

_____

_____

_____

_____

_____

_____

_____

I will try number _____ .   If that doesn't work, I will try number _____ .

Lack of inhibition

Pupils with AS often 'challenge' people around them because of a lack of inhibition. These actions are due to poor neural connections, which fail to suppress 'inappropriate behaviour' until the pupils are specifically taught the hidden social codes. Even then, they may reason that if you're a teacher it's not logical to want to make a mistake or leave it uncorrected.

Pupils with AS have no natural respect for authority. If you are a teacher you are expected to know your subject. If you make an error they will tell you. If you ask a question, they will give you a honest answer. Be careful about what you ask and the way you word a question.

Social situations can also be tricky, because the individual will not adhere to the unwritten rules and will say exactly what they think, regardless of the fact that they may be perceived as disrespectful, rude, or even offensive.

Pupils with AS have a strong sense of injustice and will make their feelings known. If they feel frustrated or angry they may go into meltdown and act aggressively. Avoid getting into a confrontation with them. It will only make the situation worse, especially if they feel a sense of injustice.

It is also very important never to lie to a pupil with AS because they will not understand the motivation behind it and may take it as an attempt to humiliate them. We need to remember that we are the adults and the pupil with AS has no intention of being rude or disrespectful, they are just saying it how it is. In fact, you could make them the guardian of your grammar, the police of your punctuation, the spy in the sky of your spelling…

The Bombmeter!

The Bombmeter has a 10-point scale to measure how your pupil feels at any given time. The spectrum of colours in the scale gives a visual reinforcement of the feelings. He may be in the Cool Zone (1–3) one minute and heading into meltdown, the Hot Zone (10), the next. Establish with your SENCo when it is acceptable to remove your pupil to a safe place, be it a 7 or 8. I would recommend removal at 8 initially, whatever anyone says.

Teach the pupil to use the Bombmeter to indicate to you how they are feeling. Establish how long you are going to stay out of the classroom: 10 to 15 minutes, before you return. It should also be made clear whether the pupil is expected to catch up with any work missed. The pupil should use their exit card and leave the class. You may have an area where you can sit quietly or go for a walk (not recommended if they have a habit of running away), or have a drink of water or do some calming exercises.

Make your own Bombmeter using magnetized strips covered in spectrum paper. The bomb: glue a black, rubber, ball valve washer to a metal washer with a piece of 3 cm long string inserted between them. Fray the loose end and paint it red.

The Big Bombmeter

Pupils with AS may find mornings – getting ready for school and the journey to school – very stressful. Use the big Bombmeter to gauge anxiety levels before registration and discuss any concerns before the start of the school day.

Unstructured time at breaks and lunchtimes can be stressful. Meltdowns may happen more frequently at these times. Distract the pupil by asking them to show you where they are on the big Bombmeter and ask them what you can do to make them feel better. Being able to talk to someone who will listen will often help to calm them down. This may shift their attention from what is causing them distress and encourage them to talk about their feelings and why they are feeling the way they do. To this end, when working as a TA, I painted a big Bombmeter vertically on a wall in the haven:

> Paint a spectrum in the shape of a thermometer on a wall: 7 colours, each 10 cm long, with a purple bulge at the bottom and red at the top. Ask the caretaker to drill 20 holes, 10 on either side of the Bombmeter, and insert rawl plugs; and ask the Technology Department to cut out 10 cm diameter circles in thin mdf (2 per bomb). Paint both sides black. Cut lengths of old rope, fray it at both ends and insert one end between 2 of the circles and glue together firmly. Paint the loose end red and ask the Technology Department to insert blunt end screws through the middle so that they can be pushed into the rawl plugs.

Shutdown: autistic catatonia

Most people have heard of the term meltdown in relation to ASCs. However, there is also what is known as Shutdown or Autistic Catatonia. Autistic Catatonia is a serious condition. The brain shuts down, unable to cope any more and the individual literally cannot do anything, no matter how much they want to. It may be caused by stress, anxiety or sensory overload. It is most commonly found in adolescents and young adults.

Look out for the following:

- slowing down of movement and verbal responses;
- difficulty starting or finishing actions;
- inability to act unless prompted;
- what looks like a lack of motivation or willingness to do anything;
- excessive tiredness due to reversal of day and night;
- hand tremors, rolling eyes, stiff posture, twitching and unusual posture and appearing physically frozen;
- excitement or agitation;
- an increase in repetitive, ritualistic behaviour.

> Ahmed, age 15, was taken by his mother to meet his career officer for the first time. She had prepared for the visit and he was quite happy.
>
> As soon as they entered the office Ahmed complained that the lights were too bright and the air conditioning heating system was too loud. The career officer switched both off but it was too late.
>
> Ahmed began stuttering, was unable to organize his thoughts and answer any questions coherently. He told his mother he couldn't think, and shut down, unable to communicate. She let him recover for a while on a sofa in the sunlight before taking him home.
>
> He went into shutdown due to sensory overload and anxiety about meeting a stranger for the first time.
>
> The appointment was rescheduled and when they went to the office for the second visit the lights and heating system were both off and Ahmed was able to focus on his new career officer and the interview went well.

Strategies

Once you have assessed the behaviour as being autistic catatonia, take the pupil to a sensory room or sick room to lie down quietly and recover.

In extreme cases you may simply have to cover the pupil with a coat and leave them where they are for a while until they have recovered enough to respond to gentle prompting to go to another room. Always inform the parent/carer of an episode.

- Use as few words as possible.
- Keep checking on the pupil periodically.
- They may appear to be asleep but, in my experience, they usually hear everything, so be careful what you say in their hearing range.
- Do not be surprised if your attempts to rouse them don't work – they are not sleeping but in a catatonic state.
- Remember that the mind has shut down because it simply cannot cope any more. Tolerance and understanding are needed.

Meltdown

A major concern of anyone who lives or works with a child with an ASC is the meltdown. Meltdown is not to be confused with a tantrum. A meltdown is a neurological response to stress caused by the amygdala reflex.

Tantrum	Meltdown	Signs of approaching meltdown
Goal driven.	Overwhelmed.	Zones out of their environment.
Checks to see if you are noticing.	Doesn't care whether you react or not.	Distraction – cannot concentrate.
Will take care not to get hurt.	No concern for their own or others' safety.	Muscle tension.
Calculating – will manipulate the social situation to their benefit.	No interest or awareness of the situation.	Can't speak coherently, stutters, echolalia, can't speak at all.
Will end when the goal is achieved or when situation is resolved.	Meltdown will continue until it has run its course; nothing will stop it.	Attempts to block out sensory stimuli, e.g. covers ears, closes eyes, rocks.
Child in control.	Child not in control.	Clenches fists, jaw and may grind teeth.

By the time a pupil with AS is in secondary school they can probably tell you what is likely to cause a meltdown and have some strategies to manage it. Meltdowns are more likely to happen when they are stressed and there will be clear warning signs.

Find out from parents or the primary school what the individual's 'Tell' signs are. These are physical indicators that alert you to their distress: a clenched fist, leg shaking, rocking, tense muscles.

Myles and Southwick (2005) outline three stages: Rumbling, Rage and Recovery. During the Rumbling stage there is the potential to avert a meltdown, so knowing your pupil's Tell signs is invaluable. The cues may be: body tension, fidgeting, grimacing, destroying their work, mumbling under their breath, calling out, refusing to do as they are told, a change in volume of their voice up or down, tapping a foot or hand. There are clear differences between a tantrum and a meltdown.

If you are aware that a meltdown is imminent, there are several things you can do:

- Discreetly acknowledge that they are distressed by moving close to them and touching the fidgeting hand or leg (make sure they can see this coming but also be aware that a light touch may be physically painful).
- Physically place yourself between your target pupil and the person who is causing distress, if it is another pupil or even the teacher, so that they cannot distract them.
- Direct their attention away from what is upsetting them by getting them to focus on their work.
- Use a sensory box with tactile objects that will calm the pupil; some smells can have a soothing effect.
- Distract them using their interest, humour, food and drink.
- When it becomes clear that the pupil has lost all concentration and is too stressed, prevent a meltdown by removing them from the room to a quiet room or sensory room.
- Remove them from the room to do a favourite activity, which will distract and engage the senses and calm them.

Kylie is aged 12. The noise levels were rising in the lesson. Kylie shifted in the chair, frowning and glaring at another pupil who was talking loudly to their partner. Muscles tensed and fists closed. The TA scribbled the outline of a big spider on her note pad and asked, 'Have I got this right?' The pupil looked at the picture. 'The eyes are all wrong and it's got 8 legs!' The TA moved her pencils and crayons across and Kylie coloured it in, concentrating hard on the detail, which helped to block out the overwhelming noise. They stayed in class for the whole lesson.

Further reading

Myles, B.S. and Southwick, J. (2005). *Asperger Syndrome and Difficult Moments: Practical solutions for tantrums, rage and meltdowns*. 2nd revised edition. Autism Asperger Publishing Co.

In meltdown

The Rage stage can be very upsetting for all involved and may include physical violence against themselves, others or property. It can be emotional and loud or the pupil may withdraw and be unable to communicate at all, falling into a catatonic state. Some have described it as similar to an epileptic episode.

Do not:
- get into an argument with the pupil;
- try to assert your authority;
- issue threats;
- raise your voice;
- kettle them (trap them in a corner or lock them in a room);
- use physical force unless it is to protect the pupil or others from harm.

Do:
- avoid any other provocation that may make the situation worse.

Enabling the pupil to gain control is different from the adult controlling the situation. The former is achievable, the latter is not, because once a meltdown has started it has to run its course. Having lost all inhibition, at this stage they will not respect rank nor reason.

So what do you do when a meltdown occurs?

Strategies for managing meltdowns

- **Stay calm.** It is far more distressing for the person in meltdown than it is for you. They are totally overwhelmed.
- If you aren't the pupil's key worker, who they trust, send for them or someone else to discreetly support you, especially if the pupil is likely to run.
- Other members of staff should not intervene, unless it is the key worker, who should take over and direct the Recovery period, it is a matter of keeping the pupil from hurting themselves or others, including you.
- If you can get to a quiet, familiar place, say, 'Follow me', in a confident tone (do not shout), and go there.
- If you touch them lightly to attract their attention, be aware that hypersensitivity may cause a violent reaction but it may also distract them. Use your judgement in respect of the pupil you are with.
- Refusal to follow is likely to be because the individual cannot process the instruction. They simply may not hear it.
- In this situation calmly remove all unnecessary people from the room.
- Sit to the side of the pupil, not opposite them, and just wait quietly.
- If they curl up on the floor under a table or huddle in a corner and rock gently – let them.
- Do not stand over them in a threatening manner, march up and down the room, or criticize their behaviour.
- Some respond to calming techniques like, 'Close your eyes. Take a deep breath in, hold, breathe out; breathe in, hold, breathe out…' This may only work in a pre-meltdown stage, when they can still hear you.
- As you see them relax you may be able to help them regain control with a favourite pastime by putting a sketch pad, character cards, magazine or book within reach.
- Some meltdowns can be destructive – be prepared for this. Tony Attwood (2006) recommends having paper they can tear up, plastic bottles or drink cans to crush.
- If they run off, follow discreetly at a distance, unless they are likely to leave the school premises and be at risk. In that situation, close the distance, explain why you need them to return to school in a calm voice and suggest a place they can be alone and safe.
- If you were the person with them at the outset, let another trusted member of staff step in and take over. The change of person may register and help calm the pupil down.
- When talking to someone in meltdown, use a low voice, speak slowly and clearly using as few words as possible, and do not comment on the incident.
- The pupil will be embarrassed. Acknowledge that you know they were upset and praise them for calming down.
- Avoid a patronising tone but use short sentences so that they understand.

A meltdown can erupt out of nowhere or build up over the day. It can last for a few seconds, several minutes or longer. Remember a meltdown is a neurobiological response, not a tantrum.

Recovery and reflection

After they have calmed down don't talk through the incident. Revisit it at another time when the pupil is able to do so in a calm manner. They may not be able to recall what happened and it could trigger another meltdown if distressed further.

If they ask you a question like, 'Am I in trouble?' reassure them they are not.

Stay in the haven, allow them to calm down and get back into the routine as soon as possible; send for class work if you do not feel it is appropriate to return to lessons. Getting back into the usual routine can be helpful, especially if the subject is of interest. Ask the pupil, 'History now?'

It is important to identify what triggered the meltdown and how they might manage the situation in future. If there are any witnesses, have them write an account of what they saw.

Consider the following:

- the environment – space, noise levels, lighting or voice;
- people – attitudes, expectations, pair or group work, bullying;
- teaching style – lecture, independent study, practicals, activity requiring self-organization, planning and execution of task, reading texts, criticism;
- classwork – lack of understanding, lack of differentiation, too easy/too hard, revision, errors, time, homework;
- sensory issues – wet clothes, smells, sounds, crowding;
- change in routine – new teacher, different room, unexpected change in anything;
- medical problem – feeling unwell or sick? This is often overlooked – check.

Use the following to assess the causes of the meltdown or any other behaviours:

The Stress Management Chart: identifies triggers and Tell signs leading up to a meltdown.

The Behaviour Assessment Chart: a quick tick box format for tracking behaviour over weeks to determine a pattern of person, place or time of day as a likely trigger. If difficulties occur during transition from one lesson to another put 'T' in the lesson box they have just left.

Behaviour Assessment Incident Record: records individual incidents in detail.

Pupil Self-Assessment Form: don't forget to involve the pupil. A simple list of questions may help you to determine their feelings and what they feel supports them and what causes the most anxiety during the day, both in lessons and at break times.

If there is a major issue with behaviour, discuss it with the SENCo and conduct an assessment of the issues across the whole experience of school life. Comprehensive strategies for dealing with the behaviour should be applied universally and consistently by all staff to lessen the impact of these distressing episodes on the target pupil, their peers, indeed the whole school.

Template 9.2 Stress Management Chart

Name of pupil:...................... Form:.................. Date:..................

Date	Time	Place	Subject	Staff present	Trigger	Distress signals	Calming Strategies

Template 9.3 Behaviour Assessment Chart – to Discern Patterns and Outcomes of Behaviour

Name:............ Form:............ Date:............ TA initials:............

Week beginning:

Behaviour Outcomes	Periods	Monday					Tuesday					Wednesday					Thursday					Friday				
		1	2	3	4	5	1	2	3	4	5	1	2	3	4	5	1	2	3	4	5	1	2	3	4	5
Teacher Initials																										
Support Staff Initials																										
Subject																										
Stops their learning																										
Affects other pupils' learning																										
Makes excessive demands on staff																										
Isolates them from their peers																										
Places pupil/s in danger																										
Outside classroom/Transition (T)																										

Week beginning:

Behaviour Outcomes	Periods	Monday					Tuesday					Wednesday					Thursday					Friday				
		1	2	3	4	5	1	2	3	4	5	1	2	3	4	5	1	2	3	4	5	1	2	3	4	5
Teacher Initials																										
Support Staff Initials																										
Subject																										
Stops their learning																										
Affects other pupils' learning																										
Makes excessive demands on staff																										
Isolates them from their peers																										
Places pupil/s in danger																										
Outside classroom/Transition (T)																										

Template 9.4 Behaviour Assessment Incident Record

Name:................ Form:................ Date:................ TA initials:................

Behaviour Outcomes	Date:	Staff Initials:	Subject:	Room:
Stops learning				
Interferes with other pupils' learning				
Isolates them from their peers				
Makes excessive demands on staff				
Reduces opportunities for involvement in ordinary school activities				
Places pupil/s in danger				

Template 9.5 Pupil Self-Assessment Form

Name:................................. Date:................................. TA initials:.................................

What were you doing at the time?			
The work was............................ I felt	Easy Happy	OK Bored	Hard Frustrated
	Too Little	Enough	Too much
Time to finish the task			
Time for your break			
Support from Teacher			
Support from TA			
The other pupils were (tick the box)	helpful	annoying	distracting
Was the feedback from the teacher...?	praise	critical	helpful
Help?	To help me you could have:		

Self-evaluation of practice

Self-evaluation is a natural part of the education process and I believe that recognizing a mistake and the need to modify our actions and behaviour is half way to solving the problem. This is especially true when working with pupils with AS who may not react in the way you might expect. Stereotyping pupils with a condition like autism is an easy trap to fall into and it is a common saying: 'If you've met one person with autism, you've met one person with autism.' They are individuals and vastly different from each other in their abilities, needs, the way they communicate, socialize, behave, process their environment and learn. Working with pupils with AS means that we have to come to the job with open minds and a willingness to learn, be flexible and adapt to their needs.

It is useful to assess the role we play when pupils with AS cannot manage their behaviour, and consider the following:

- **We are part of the problem:** for example, we did not modify language; the task was not broken down; we insisted on eye contact; we made the pupil work in a group; or even we were in a bad mood…
- **We did not take action early enough:** for example, we failed to remove the pupil from the classroom when showing signs of distress and/or sensory overload; we did not prevent another pupil from being annoying to the pupil with AS; we failed to notice the pupil struggling with the task.
- **We made the situation worse with our intervention:** for example, we interrupted the pupil with AS while they were talking or concentrating; we took control of a situation when someone else was dealing with it; we raised our voice.
- **We made a mistake that caused a reaction with this particular pupil:** for example, wearing perfume; using a particular colour as background to a display; or studying a particular topic that could be a phobia for this pupil.

It is important to learn what we should not do, because that will inform any action we may take. Equally, it's helpful to establish what action or behaviour supports and reassures the pupil, and this information should be included on the pupil passport. Everyone who works with the pupil should communicate regularly and this can be done through the use of the comms book.

To analyze the incident, I favour the ABC method for both pupils and staff..

ABC stands for:
Antecedent – what happened leading up to the problem behaviour?
Behaviour – the observed problem behaviour.
Consequence – the event, which immediately follows the response.

Example 1
Antecedent – Teacher asks Amy to get on with her work.
Behaviour – Amy swears and throws work on the floor.
Consequence – Teacher sends her out of the lesson.

Regular observations of Amy may identify that the function of this behaviour is to enable her to avoid doing her class work. The reason? She's in a bad mood or she finds the work too hard and needs help to understand and complete the task.

Example 2
Antecedent – the class is noisy because pupils are chatting.
Behaviour – Teacher shouts at class to be quiet.
Consequence – Tom, a pupil with AS, who wasn't talking, becomes agitated and distressed and leaves the lesson.

Regular observations may identify that Tom becomes extremely anxious when teachers shout in lessons and consequently it would be helpful for teachers to modify their behaviour to help him stay in class.

It may also be useful to consider the following as hidden antecedents:

- Changes in routine: timetable, room, teacher or TA, which may have taken place earlier in the day. If so, was the pupil alerted to the changes in advance? How far in advance? Does the pupil need visual support to alert them to a change?
- Was there a report of any concerns prior to the pupil coming to school, the lesson or the incident, from parents, other teachers or TAs?

Things to consider regarding one's own behaviour are:

- Did I modify my language?
- Was the task differentiated to meet the pupil's needs and enable them to complete the task?
- Did the pupil understand what was expected of him or her?
- Were there any sensory issues?
- Do I know the signs the pupil displays when getting distressed?
- If so, what was my response? Was it appropriate? Did it make the situation better or worse?

Pause for thought…

- What sort of mood am I in today – did this come across to the pupil?
- Do I know enough about ASCs to react appropriately to the pupil's needs?
- Do I know about the characteristics of this pupil's ASC and their specific needs?
- Does this pupil trust me to have their best interests at heart? Do I have a good relationship with this pupil? (This is very important with pupils with an ASC as they need to feel they are accepted and respected and to feel safe and competent.)
- What can I do to ensure this does not happen again?

Discuss the incident with the pupil after it is over, when they are calm and rational. They may be able to help you understand the reasons for their behaviour and what would be a helpful way to respond that calms the situation and allows the pupil to feel safe and competent and effects a better outcome in future.

It is worth noting that, contrary to popular belief, children with ASCs are very empathetic, indeed overly so, and may pick up on a mood, nuance or atmosphere very quickly. After all, they have to notice the smallest of clues that tell the truth of the matter, due to detail focus processing. Their cool reaction in situations, where you would expect a more emotional response, is because they don't know what to do about it or what to say. It doesn't mean they don't feel things deeply – especially anything they feel is unjust or may humiliate them.

Template 9.6 ABC Analysis

Name:.. Observer:..

Date		Time		Place		Present	

Antecedent	
Behaviour	
Consequence	
Possible function of the behaviour	
Proposed modifications to behaviour	

10 Discipline and pupils with AS

Disciplining pupils with AS is contentious because AS is a neuro-physiological disorder. 'Bad' behaviour may be a result of the condition. A meltdown is often when it occurs. In this state they rarely know what's happening or what they are doing. It can be frightening. They may kick a door so hard it breaks, lash out at another pupil or throw a chair across a room. It's distressing for everybody, especially the pupil with AS, who may not be conscious of what is happening until it is all over.

Establish the cause. If it is a sensory overload, disciplining the pupil is inappropriate; schools need to take responsibility to meet the needs of pupils with AS. If it was frustration, for example, and the pupil rejects help and goes into meltdown, then there should be consequences. Autism explains the behaviour but does not excuse it.

However, what those consequences should be is another matter. We need to consider what we mean by consequences. Are consequences punishment or outcomes? Often the pupil with AS does not react to punishment in the way we would expect. Punishment is often used as a deterrent but this is only effective if the pupil knows what will happen if they do something and the punishment is something they don't want to do. To be sent out of a noisy lesson is not really a punishment for a pupil who is experiencing sensory overload or sees the lesson as pointless. Also every occasion is perceived as a unique experience, so the pupil may not learn the 'lesson' and behave better next time because no two experiences are necessarily the same. However, NTs may see it that way if the same 'bad behaviour' occurs again in the same subject, same room and with the same teacher. It may be a sunny day on the first occasion and a rainy day the next, so in the autistic mind it is completely different.

Often in schools punishments are reactive: the pupil does something the teacher finds objectionable, therefore the teacher decides to punish them. The punishment is then decided on the spot and handed out, usually a detention during lunch, break or after school, or internal exclusion whereby the pupil is removed from the lesson and sent to the exclusion room to work for the rest of the day.

When I have accompanied a pupil with AS to the exclusion room, I have asked them why they thought they were being excluded from lessons. Rarely was it understood as being a punishment for a particular action. As such, the punishment is ineffective and will not be a deterrent. The pupil has not understood why their behaviour is unacceptable because no-one has explained it to them.

Unlike typical children, who may do things out of badness, the child with AS generally won't. That doesn't mean to say that they don't do bad things – but their motivation for doing them is different. Their inability to predict what is going to happen next with any reasonable accuracy creates anxiety, distress and fear. At these times the need to control the situation may be overwhelming. Under these circumstances, a child with AS may reason that if they act in a certain way then the teacher will react in a predictable manner, and they derive some comfort from knowing what will happen. The problem arises when that action is bad behaviour that causes the teacher to shout and reprimand the pupil. Without understanding the motives behind the action, we make the assumption that the pupil is deliberately behaving badly, being rude or manipulative rather than anxious or distressed, especially when the pupil smiles or 'smirks' upon achieving the desired reaction.

The school will have a set of rules. The pupil with AS will either:

- follow the rules to the letter and tell on anyone who doesn't;
- or flout any rule they see as being stupid and tell you so.

When they have calmed down after an incident, ask them to write their account to help you understand why it happened. They will usually tell the truth even if it shows them to be wrong. However, they may be too distressed to do this the same day. Use a comic conversation and draw the incident.

Their version of what happened may be enlightening. Do not dismiss a totally outlandish explanation as a pack of lies. Remember that the way the pupil with AS perceives the world is completely different from yours. They may see the behaviour as perfectly logical.

What next? Exclusion is the conventional approach. Is it the most effective? The pupil needs to learn what is inappropriate behaviour and how to exercise self-discipline.

An extraordinary letter of apology

Once a decision has been made that there should be consequences for their actions, it is important to inform the pupil as soon as possible. Nothing could be worse for them than waiting, not knowing what is going to happen. Much anxiety caused by attending mainstream schools is from not knowing what is going to happen next. Inform them when the intervention is going to take place, where and with whom. The pupil's key worker with whom they have a good relationship and who they trust is the ideal person.

An Extraordinary Letter of Apology is a strategy designed to help secondary school pupils with AS recognize the bad behaviour, acknowledge the effect their actions have on others and show appropriate alternatives. Having autism makes it difficult for someone with AS to imagine these – we need to show them.

- When? When they have calmed down, the next day or later.
- Where? If applying sanctions, the internal exclusion room, otherwise a quiet room.
- Who with? Key worker – someone they trust.

Resources

- Account of the incident – a scrupulously, accurate narrative.
- Paper.
- Pens – including red, green, orange and blue.

Have the pupil:

1   Read the account.
2   In green, tick when someone tried to help, for example by asking 'Would you like time out?' Or picking up something they threw down.
3   In red, place a cross when they behaved badly, for example, spoke rudely or threw something.

4   Check that every incident is acknowledged.
5   Discuss each point with the pupil, asking: Why was that the wrong thing to do? How do you think this made them feel? How would you feel if...?
6   During this stage they usually realize they have behaved badly and apologize. Reassure them. Say, 'We're going to write a letter of apology together'.
7   Go through the account with the orange pen and draw an arrow at a place where an alternative presents itself and write in blue what they could have done instead, for example, walk away.
8   The pupil writes the letter, including: acknowledgements of what they did wrong; why it was wrong; how they made the other person feel; and what they could have done instead.
9   Deliver the letter and wait for the apology to be acknowledged.
10 The person who receives the apology should simply thank them.
11 Do not reprimand them nor extract a promise not to repeat the behaviour.
12 Do not mention the incident again unless they do, or you are praising them for their understanding and apology.

11   Bullying and Asperger Syndrome

Over 40 per cent of children on the autistic spectrum have been bullied at school. The impact on children and families can be devastating. Many of the children and families we surveyed report damage to self-esteem, mental health and progress at school. Some withdraw from school altogether, others never fully recover from their experiences.

B. Reid and A. Batten (2006)

Pupils with AS generally want to make friends but lack the necessary social and communication skills and may exhibit odd behaviours, which make it difficult for them to become accepted by their peers, and this odd behaviour attracts unwanted attention. Some of the behaviours of a pupil with AS attempting to interact may be misunderstood and seen as bullying or harassment. A thoughtful gesture or kind remark made to a pupil with AS may lead them to believe they have found a friend. This 'friend' may then find themselves being 'stalked'.

Pupils with AS are socially naive and, without a group of friends to support them, they are easy victims of backhanded bullying. This involves a pupil with AS being misled to do something inappropriate, getting them into trouble: for example, getting a boy to deliver a message to a teacher in the girls' changing rooms at PE. This naivety makes it easier for bullies to appear to befriend the pupil in public, set them up either to do something inappropriate or have a meltdown, and sit back to watch the show!

Bullying a pupil with AS affects their self-esteem, mental well-being, development of social skills and any academic progress they might make in school. This is particularly prevalent among teenagers. The after-effects of bullying go on to ruin the lives of some victims, leading to problems with low self-esteem, further isolation, depression, fear and illness. They replay the event in their mind over and over again, feeling the same emotions of confusion, humiliation, impotence and despair as they did when it took place. This can lead to self-harm and suicide.

The following is an extract from research conducted by Humphrey and Symes (2011):

Robertson, Chamberlain & Kasari (2003) found that the more negative relationship teachers had with such pupils, the less socially accepted they were by their peers. This is particularly worrying as the difficulties in social interaction experienced by pupils with ASDs already put them at risk of negative social outcomes.

There is anecdotal evidence of teachers and TAs ignoring teasing and bullying, and even condoning it by suggesting the victim ignores the teasing – 'walk away and it will go away' – or that the victim should 'toughen up'. This strategy does not stop teasing and may, in fact, encourage the bullies to escalate the teasing until it becomes bullying.

People may even blame the victim for the bullying, saying that they brought it on themselves. Inappropriate action is common, for example, removing the victim from the classroom and teaching them in isolation, while the perpetrators continue to be taught in class.

Pupils with AS may not report instances of bullying, which can lead to an escalation in the bullying they suffer. Or they may report every incident of teasing or being knocked accidentally when going from one lesson to the next in crowded corridors and be regarded like the child who cried 'Wolf!' too often.

TAs working with pupils with AS are crucial to the development of positive attitudes among staff and NT pupils to those with ASCs. When working as a TA supporting pupils with AS, I was always keen to show how much I enjoyed my interaction with them. It wasn't difficult. They are remarkable individuals.

Warning: the use of sarcasm is likely to be taken literally and may lead to great upset. Avoid it in conversation with your target pupil with AS or even with the class of which they are part. Teachers may be unaware of the devastating effect it has on pupils with AS; if this is the case, please warn them that the pupil may be confused, feel stupid and targeted, and have a perception that they are being bullied. It may have a lasting effect on their self-esteem.

However, there are two parts to the problem: identifying the 'teasing' or 'bullying' as being malicious, and neutralizing it. A pupil with AS has problems assessing verbal bullying, because of their tendency to take things literally, and they will need to be taught the difference between banter and malicious bullying intended to humiliate.

Strategies for the pupil

- Teach the pupil what bullying is. Laminate the Am I Being Bullied? 'questions' (see Template 11.1). Put them on a key fob for the pupil, who can use them to assess whether they were bullied.
- Ensure the pupil understands that:
  - they are not alone
  - it is not their fault
  - no-one has the right to treat them like that.
- Encourage them to report any instances of bullying during Social Skills lessons.
- Teach the pupil one liners to say in response to verbal teasing (see Template 11.2 for suggestions).
- Ensure the pupil is not left unsupervised in areas of risk – PE changing room, toilets and the playground at break times.
- Make the disabled toilets available to them to change in and use.
- Encourage retreating to the haven when feeling threatened.
- Introduce lunchtime clubs in the pupil's area of interest: for example, chess or manga drawing. The pupil could take the lead and teach others.
- Give an Autism Awareness lesson with the form group.
- Set up a Buddy system within the form with peers who want to help, supporting the pupil with AS through the day, especially at break times.
- Establish Pupil Mentors with high status to spend time once a week with the younger pupil with AS.
- Hold Autism Awareness Assemblies for the whole school.
- Use drama to highlight problems with bullying.
- Use drama to develop skills to combat bullying.
- Empower bystanders to intervene.

Strategies for staff

- Awareness of the types of bullying that goes on among young people, including backhanded bullying (being deceived into doing something inappropriate), cyber-bullying and hazing. (Hazing is ritual humiliation, which is endured, in order to be accepted into a group.)
- Zero tolerance of bullying.
- Be patient and listen.
- Take every report of bullying seriously and investigate it.
- Never punish the pupil for behaviour related to their autism.
- Do not use sarcasm and avoid teasing.
- Play to the pupil's strengths in class.
- Class reader in English in Years 7, 8 and 9 could include the following:
  - *House Rules* by Jodi Picoult
  - *The London Eye Mystery* by Siobhan Dowd
  - *The Curious Incident of the Dog in the Night Time* by Mark Haddon (Children's Edition).
- Display a poster showing at least one person in each subject department who is an autism hero, and label them as such.
- Read Dubin's book (see below)!

Further reading

*Dubin, N. (2007). *Asperger Syndrome and Bullying Strategies and Solutions*. London: Jessica Kingsley Publishers.

Reid, B. and Batten, A. (2006). *B is for Bullied: the experience of children with autism and their families*. The National Autistic Society.

Stobart, A. (2009). *Bullying and Autism Spectrum Disorders – A guide for school staff*. The National Autistic Society.

Am I being
bullied?

Did they
hurt me
physically?

Did they
call me names?

Did I feel bad?

Was I
frightened?

Are they
lying about me?

Do they
stop me playing
with them?

Do they ignore
me when I talk
to them?

Did they
do it more than
2 times?

I must check
with somebody
I trust.

Stay Calm
and Be Cool

Really? How kind of you to let me know.

I didn't know you cared.

This is getting boring.

You're always trying to help? Thanks.

Do you feel better now?

Do I look like I care?

You talking to me again?

Shame – we could've been friends.

Enough now! Get a life!

Yeah, yeah. Whatever!

Peer interventions to combat bullying

The following are ideas for interventions to support pupils with AS in mainstream schools when they were having problems making friends. If the local authority has an Autism Outreach Team, I recommend that you contact them to advise you and help devise and/or lead any peer intervention strategies.

Autism Awareness Assembly

This can be a very effective intervention, but it must explain:

- Why the pupil with AS is different because of their brain development.
- How this affects the behaviour of the person on the autism spectrum.
- The special qualities of individuals with AS and positive role models.

This has to be done in a way that your audience understands; this could be a challenge, so if you do not have a specialist in the school, I recommend that you invite the Autism Outreach Team from your local council or a private speaker on the subject.

Buddy system

This is a tried and tested model of inclusive practice to encourage the socialization into the school community of pupils with difficulties. However, with a pupil with AS this has to be dealt with sensitively. The Buddy will not only have to be a responsible member of the school community with high status but also one who will be able to understand the particular difficulties associated with autism and be able to manage the pupil, who may be very reliant upon the 'friendship'. The pupil will have to be taught the social conventions of the peer group. It is not enough to trust they will be able to observe and imitate. I recommend a group of buddies from the pupil's class or a senior member of the school on a sports team if the pupil has an interest in a particular sport.

Often pupils with AS have a special interest or skill, which can be built up by setting up a club around the interest and encouraging the pupil to lead the group. Examples include: chess, music, drama, video gaming, raspberry pi, manga and war gaming.

If the pupil can lead the group and teach a skill it will help elevate the pupil's status and raise self-esteem. It will have to be monitored because the communication and social skills of the pupil with AS may be impaired and misunderstood.

Class project – positive role models who may have had AS

Anecdotal accounts in diaries and letters and considered observations of contemporary behaviour have led to a number of well-known figures being identified as probably having the condition. Each department could have an Aspie hero displayed on the wall as a positive message.

There are also the fictional characters: Sherlock Holmes, Dr Who, Spock and Data from *Star Trek* and Kyle Caddick (Richard Fleeshman) in *All the Small Things* (2009).

Strategy

Give each pupil one of the following people to research for a short talk on 'People who have changed the world'.

Do not tell them at this stage that these people may have been autistic.

Task:

- If possible, research how your subject was viewed as a child: many would have been regarded as obsessive, stupid, lazy, weird...
- Then research their later achievements, for a short presentation to the rest of the class.

Joy Adamson	Woody Allen	Hans Christian Andersen
W. H. Auden	Isaac Asimov	Dan Ackroyd
Ludwig van Beethoven	Alexander Bell	Pip Brown/Ladyhawke
David Bellamy	Tim Burton	Arthur C. Clarke
Lewis Carroll	Marie Curie	Leonardo da Vinci
Charles Darwin	Arthur Conan Doyle	Bob Dylan
Thomas Edison	Albert Einstein	Bobby Fischer
Henry Ford	Dian Fossey	Bill Gates
Antoni Gaudi	Darryl Hannah	Jim Henson
Alfred Hitchcock	Thomas Jefferson	Wassily Kandinsky
L.S. Lowry	Michelangelo	Mozart
Isaac Newton	Gary Numan	George Orwell
Michael Palin	Carl Sagan	George Bernard Shaw
Steven Spielberg	Satoshi Tajiri	Daniel Tammet
James Taylor	Nikola Tesla	Alan Turing
Mark Twain	Vincent van Gogh	Andy Warhol
George Washington.		

These are all people who have achieved remarkable things in their field of interest. Discuss their achievements. People with Asperger Syndrome are born with a different way of seeing the world. It's not better.... not worse.... just different.

Sometimes these differences can make a real impact. After the presentation, ask the pupils if they think 'their character' has changed the world for the rest of us and to give their reasons for their opinion.

Don't emphasize the idea of 'genius'; rather, draw attention to the fact that with Asperger Syndrome it is possible to concentrate on something for really long periods of time. Why would being able to focus on something be a good thing?

They have the imagination to create inventions, or ideas and solutions to problems, and amazing works of art and music that require so much time that the rest of us would be bored, dismayed and ready to give up.

Some examples of how 'interests' and perseverance have led to great achievements:

- Michelangelo took four years to paint the ceiling of the Sistine Chapel, from start to finish. He was absent for at least two long periods during that time but went on to paint the 'Last Judgement', which took six years.

- Spielberg made his first film for his photography badge as a boy scout aged 12, but only achieved success in 1974 with *Jaws*. Since then he has directed many films you all know. He likes to spend his free time watching films back to back.
- Arthur C. Clarke has a book catalogued in every section of the Dewey decimal library system except philosophy.
- Charles Darwin: at the age of 16 his father told him, 'You care for nothing but shooting, dogs and rat-catching, and you will be a disgrace to yourself and all your family'. He studied to be a clergyman but his hobby was natural history, especially beetles. He set out on the *Beagle* from 1831–1836 and published *On The Origin of the Species* in 1859!
- Marie Curie: in 1898, the Curies announced the existence of radium. In 1910 Marie Curie, working on without her husband, who had been killed in 1906, isolated 10 grams of pure radium metal after processing tons of pitch blend.

Savants

Savant comes from the French word *savoir*, meaning to know. Savants are people with a learning disability who have pools of extraordinary ability, like the artist Stephen Wiltshire, and Derek Paravacini the blind pianist. One in ten people with autism have some ability and 10 per cent of savants are people with autism. However, 'prodigious savants', like Daniel Tammet, mathematician, multi-linguist and author, who has Asperger Syndrome, are extremely rare. There are fewer than 100 such people in the whole world!

Luke Jackson said about television programmes about savants,

I find these television programs depressing, I got all the nerdiness and freakishness but none of the genius.

However, it has been my experience that many younger pupils in years 7 and 8 with AS are proud to be associated with them and see them as genuine role models.

There are several videos about these savants on YouTube, which you might use in an assembly or intervention:

Derek Paravacinus: The Musical Genius
Daniel Tammet: The Boy with the Incredible Brain
Beautiful Minds: Stephen Wiltshire draws a picture of Rome in 3 days.

Further Reading

*Tammet, D. (2007). *Born on a Blue Day: The gift of an extraordinary mind*. London: Hodder Paperbacks.

Peer intervention

There are a number of reasons why you might think it is a good idea to do a Peer Intervention on behalf of a pupil with AS. It may be part of the good autism practice that the school undertakes towards inclusion. Another reason may be that the pupil him or herself wishes to tell their peers that they have Asperger Syndrome and explain their behaviour because they are aware of the impact that their idiosyncrasies have on their desire to make friends and be accepted for who they are.

The other motivation resulting in a Reactive Peer Intervention may be that staff have witnessed that the relationship between the pupil with AS and their peers is deteriorating at such a rate because of their odd behaviour that they are in danger of being totally ostracized and isolated by their peers, and this may lead to bullying. This is to be avoided at all costs because the impact on the self-esteem of the pupil can lead to a negative effect on their academic achievement, and, at the very worst, tragic consequences.

However, this has to be dealt with very sensitively, with regard to the feelings of both the pupil with AS and his or her parents. Many parents do not want it known that their child has an autism spectrum condition, and you must respect their wishes. Their motivation is that they fear for their child and the attention they might attract from it being generally known they are on the spectrum. Some parents, who acknowledge that they are on the spectrum themselves, may have had terrible experiences at school; therefore, a peer intervention has to be a joint undertaking.

If the school initiates the intervention it needs to be discussed with the key TA and the form tutor. They may be able to highlight any issues that might arise concerning the pupil and their peers. Do not mention it to the pupil before speaking to the parents. Some pupils may be unaware that they have Asperger Syndrome. Invite the parents in to discuss the intervention and explain why you consider it to be necessary.

Once you have the agreement of the parents, tell them what you intend to do and how. Invite them to help their child put the presentation together. Go through your contribution to the presentation with the parents so that they understand exactly what you are going to do and are reassured that this is not going to humiliate their son or daughter. I do not recommend that parents attend the intervention with the class. The pupil may be very anxious and this may add to their distress. Reassure the pupil that they have the right to withdraw from their part in the intervention and that you will support them at every moment during the talk.

Henry, aged 13, broke down at the start of his talk. The TA, who was supporting him, turned him to face her, side on to the class, and directed him to talk to her. Turning away from the class and looking at her he was able to continue and completed his talk. He soon regained his self-confidence and was able to turn to face the class and answered their questions confidently.

If there is another pupil with AS, who has done this before and would like to help, invite them to give advice and support. It will reassure the pupil giving the talk and also raise the self-esteem of both pupils.

Asperger Syndrome and me: Peer Intervention strategy

1   Keep the format simple – a PowerPoint presentation is helpful because it allows photographs to be used to illustrate the 'text'.
2   Split the presentation into two parts: the pupil and the condition.
3   **Part 1**: the pupil with AS gives a talk about themselves to their form, introducing themselves:
    a. My name is *****.
    b. I have a sister/brother, who is a pain… (usually), a dog and a cat.
    c. My interests are … military history and restoring old minis. Here is a photo of me with my dad at a mini rally at Goodwood last year. It took us two years to put this car back together!

    d. The best holiday I had was... because...

    e. My favourite subjects are...

    f. And finally: My name is ***** and I have Asperger Syndrome. I have a different operating system.

4   The idea is that they are just kids with similar interests to everyone else but...

5   **Part 2**: an adult explains what Asperger Syndrome is: a difference in the way the brain is formed (use the analogy of the road system on page 7 to explain the way it works).

6   Explain how this can lead to difficulties in communication and misunderstanding.

7   There are two main areas of behaviour to explain: lack of inhibition and sensory overload.

8   Option – show videos from YouTube (see below).

9   Finally, mention some of the more gifted people with AS, like Bill Gates and Steve Jobs, that the peers can relate to, and point out that while it's difficult in school, people like ***** could change the world.

10 Ask the peers to help provide support for the pupil during the school day, and explain the Buddy system.

Videos

BBC Newsround: My Autism and Me: Rosie http://www.youtube.com/watch?v=ejpWWP1HNGQ

Dean Beadle: an extract from his talk in Cardiff in which he describes his impulsive behaviour – running away from his mother in the supermarket with the shopping trolley in his 20s. Very funny and illustrates the lack of self-control. Will need editing. http://www.youtube.com/watch?v=LC0JytWaQZM

Part Three

12   High Stakes Examinations

Training for high stakes examinations (GCSEs and GCEs) needs to begin in Year 7. The language used is generic and should, therefore, be noted on the Key Words page from the outset. Subject teachers should use key words consistently and give the pupil with AS a handout with the definitions – what they mean in an examination context – for easy reference. Keep a copy in a folder.

Other areas of difficulty are showing workings in Maths answers and effective scrutiny and commentary of pictures, diagrams, graphs and other illustrations, due to detail focus processing. Select a method, teach it and be consistent.

I recommend that the pupil with AS is familiarised with the format of the examination paper well in advance of the examination. If the examination paper offers choices they will need to be taught how to navigate it efficiently by using the index. The terms used by examination boards still have potential for misinterpretation and the pupil with need to be able to decode these. Prepare them for any eventuality. Remember, if they are stressed they are likely to take everything literally.

> Jason, aged 16, was unable to pass beyond the blank page, which read, 'This page has been left blank intentionally'. The invigilator noticed his distress and when asked what was wrong was told, "The page isn't blank. Why do they say it's blank? That's wrong". He was unable to continue in spite of the invigilator's explanation and reassurances.

A word of warning: ensure that the pupil with AS understands that there will be 'practice' or mock exams. Pupils on the spectrum have been known to refuse to do an examination if they have already done it and 'passed'. It is important to explain when and where the real examinations take place and what happens to the papers.

They need to be told that the examiner, who marks the papers, will only be able to give marks for what is on the paper. This is particularly important if you have a pupil who does not need to go through the stages to arrive at an answer. Translate the number of marks given into sections of the answer.

They will have to be directed to answering the question fully by noting the number of marks awarded for this answer. Don't guess; have a look at the mark schemes online at the examination board's website and show it to the pupil. Then they will know exactly what is expected of them.

Maths examinations can be difficult for the pupil with AS, who is able to do complex equations in their head. Some may not be able to tell you how they arrived at the answer. It is therefore important that you train them to go through each question step by step.

Teach your pupil how to answer examination questions:

1   Read the question carefully.
2   What does the question tell me to do? Write down the key words. Or highlight them on the paper.

3   Plan the answer, using the PEEL template format. There is no reason why it cannot be drawn in the examination answer booklet.
4   Begin with an opening sentence paraphrasing the question in order to refocus on a direct answer to the question.
5   Pay attention to Maths examinations and the need to get all the working out down as evidence that the candidate understands the method as well as the answer.

Key Words

Of paramount importance is decoding the language used in examinations. Teachers should train pupils with AS from Year 7 to interpret the **key words** used in high stakes examinations.
    'When you see (this word) – Write about …'
    '*Comment* on the writer's use of language' = Write about; and list the points the pupil needs to cover in response to this instruction.
    Take nothing for granted when it comes to the level of understanding of your pupil.
    Ask the Head of Department to make a glossary of terms relating to the examination questions from past papers and have this in your folder for easy reference.

When scribing for an AS pupil in a mock examination, the task: 'Comment on the writer's use of language' elicited the response 'He's writing in American English because he is American'. And that was it: the whole answer and, being an exam, nothing I could do about it. The pupil interpreted the word language literally.

Top Tip

Note 'Key Words' for each lesson on A4 paper (with definitions) until the pupil recognizes what they mean in the context of coursework and examinations.

Workmats

Workmats may support a variety of topics in lessons. To avoid confusion, use images to illustrate key words for topics in subjects, for example the water cycle, with images taken from the text book or PowerPoint the teacher uses in class.
    Place images and definitions around the perimeter of the mat, with a space for the exercise book in the middle.

Text workmats (using Microsoft Publisher)

Format the page into Landscape. (This is an effective way of supporting the study of a poem.)
    Place the text in the centre of the page using a single column for A4 or double columns for A3.
    Arrange the illustrations around the perimeter of the page.
    Draw coloured boxes around the illustration and underline the text relating to the picture in the same colour (see opposite).

Template 12.1

Red

Red

Red

Purple

Purple

Purple

Text relates to the diagrams or pictures in the boxes by matching the colour of the font to the colour of the boxes.

Using corners with separate colours will also help with the visual perception of the ordering of theme of the content

Green

Green

Green

Blue

Blue

Blue

13   Organization: practicalities

The super-organized individual with AS may insist on everything being in its right place as a way of controlling their environment. Let them organize their workspace as they want. It is discreet ritual and preventing it may cause distress.

Or they may be utterly hopeless at organization, leaving their things all over the school then getting anxious because they can't find anything and will get into trouble. Be very patient and reassuring. Helping the pupils with AS organize themselves at school is one of the key tasks because it reduces levels of anxiety.

Before the pupil arrives in school, getting them out of bed and the safety of their room to go to the noisy, confusing and stressful environment of school may be a daily battle for parents. It is likely that they will have to be reminded to do basic things every day. They may be highly 'organized' at home, with instructions displayed telling them what to do to prepare for the day: how to wash, which clothes to wear, what things to put in their schoolbag. Parents may use a visual reference like Communicate in Print (Widgit) or Picture Set symbols to reinforce the message.

Top Tip

Find out the level of organizational support given at home to use as a baseline for support given in school. It will reassure the pupil and increase their trust that you understand and are genuinely trying to help. Be discreet. Never criticize them for their difficulties with organization. It won't change anything, just lower their self-esteem. Put strategies in place to help them.

Strategies

- Arrange for PE gear to be put somewhere safe at the beginning of the day and return it to the same place at the end of the lesson.
- Remind the pupil to take the kit home to be washed at regular intervals.
- Colour code the timetable – match the colour of subject to the colour of the exercise books used in that subject.
- Fill in the homework diary using the same subject colour codes, highlighting when the homework must be done and when it must be handed in. They should be encouraged to do this for themselves. They may insist on doing the homework the night before it is due to be handed in.
- Symbols may be used to illustrate subjects and instructions; for example, an open book for doing the homework and a closed one for handing it in.
- Have a checklist of equipment required for the lesson on a key fob for easy reference, or use a Workmat with illustrations.

- Use the Practical Subjects template (which you can find at the end of Chapter 20) to help the pupil focus on how to organize.
- Establish a routine for preparing for a lesson – see example key fob on Template 13.1.
- Include all equipment necessary for what they are learning in PE: mouth guard, shin pads, gloves… and support with images if necessary.
- Note any regular after school clubs, supported with appropriate symbols denoting the activity, be it sport, drama or music…

Websites

Communicate in Print 2: http://www.widgit.com/products/inprint/index.htm

Picture Set, Special Education Technology: British Columbia, Ministry of Education Provincial Resource Program: http://www.setbc.org/pictureset/Default.aspx

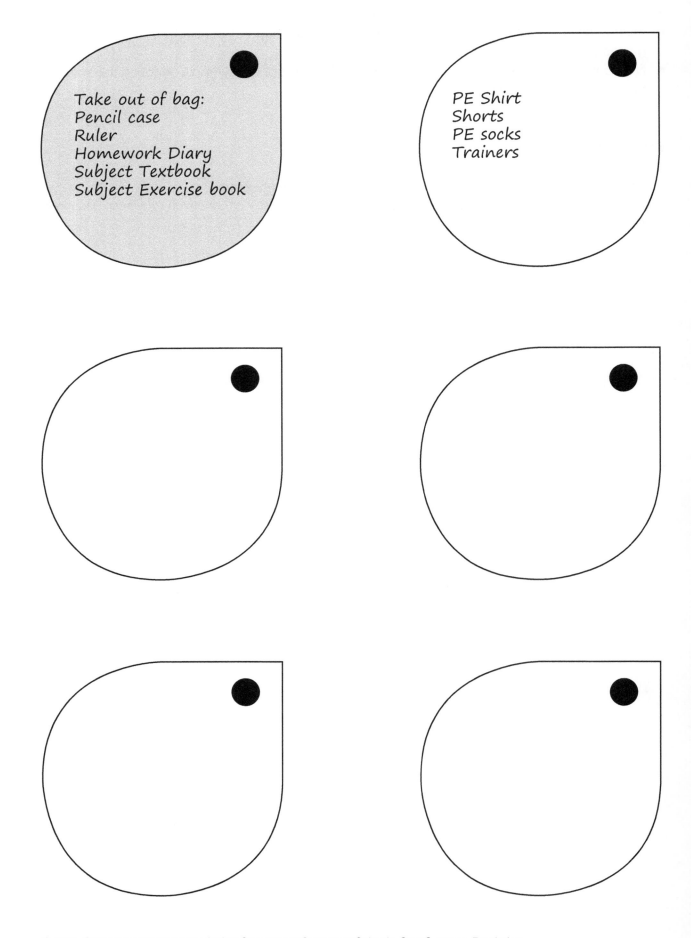

Take out of bag:
Pencil case
Ruler
Homework Diary
Subject Textbook
Subject Exercise book

PE Shirt
Shorts
PE socks
Trainers

Questions to ask when supporting the pupil with AS in organizing their work

- 'What did Mrs Collins tell you to do?'
- 'What materials will you need?'
- 'What will you do first?'
- 'What will you do after that?'
- 'What will you do when you have finished?'

Don't ask the next question until you have received an answer to the previous one and allow time for processing.

Remember your words don't travel round the brain in a direct path and the pupil with an ASC may need time to process what you have said.

You could write the questions down on a key fob. After a while the pupil may learn what to do without prompting but it will take time.

Top Tip

Do not alter the wording of your question. Repeat it again, after a suitable interval, using exactly the same words.

14 Autism is a communication difficulty

Communication is around 20 per cent verbal and 80 per cent body language. Add to that the ability to understand the intention of the speaker, or being able to 'read between the lines', and you begin to understand the level of skill required to communicate. This is a set of skills people with an ASC have to be taught carefully and repeatedly and may never use effectively.

Cognition is the mental action or process of acquiring knowledge and understanding through thought, experience and the senses. Cognitive processing is a much bigger challenge for pupils with AS than we appreciate. Research has shown that people with autism have to harness an extra area of the brain to try and make sense of things we take for granted. It's hard work. By the end of the day the pupil may be exhausted.

Another problem may be the inability to retain information that has just been given and relate it to the task set. NT brains can hold information that is not required at that moment but which they will need later during the task. When needed, it is retrieved effortlessly. This is called a working memory. It's like all the ingredients of a recipe laid out on a tray ready for you to use as and when needed. The brain of someone with AS will not have a full tray of ingredients; they will have forgotten to put them all out or not even realize something is needed; or they may put the ingredients together out of sequence as set out in the recipe.

Question: 'How do you like instructions presented to you?'

Answer: 'Like the ones they do for Lego and Bionicles.'

Those instructions are purely visual. There is not a word in sight.

Top Tip

Write the task down (with illustrations/symbols) one step at a time. Use numbering and/or the key fob template to maintain the order of the task. Use the least number of words possible.

Literacy and maths

It is a popular myth that all pupils with AS are brilliant at maths. This is not necessarily so. The English component of the questions can be particularly confusing. Modern maths requires a high level of literacy and knowledge of mathematical vocabulary. Language in maths can cause major difficulties because many of the terms have completely different meanings in everyday usage: for example, face means the front part of a person's head from the forehead to the chin, or the corresponding part in an animal; but in geometry it refers to each of the surfaces of a solid, the faces of a cube; mean equals miserly; in maths it refers to the average of a set of numbers (i.e. add all of the numbers and divide by how many numbers there are).

Mathematical symbols representing ideas or processes are easier for a pupil on the spectrum to decipher.

However, the terms used for one concept are numerous. Let's take the idea of:
— minus, subtract, take away, what's the difference between, less than, left with, remainder, deduct, reduce, decrease. Can you think of any more?

So instead of 10 – 4 = 6
We have: What is 10 minus/subtract/deduct/take away/less than?
Or: What is the difference between 10 and 4?
Or: Reduce/decrease 10 by 4
The minus sign is also used as a negative, e.g. – 4° C.

We tend to take it for granted that these terms are interchangeable but for the pupil with AS these synonyms simply create confusion.

Another problem is that many pupils with AS will insist on using the first method they were taught to do a calculation. You will have to persuade the pupil that the new method is the best through logic – speed and efficiency – they'll get the sum done more quickly.

Another difficulty is the use of language in modern maths. It is no longer about being able to do calculations: you have to be able to understand the instructions. Teach the mathematical terms used in examinations from Year 7.

A dictionary of mathematical terms would be a useful resource.

The problem with maths problems

Maths can be particularly problematical when answering questions with multiple parts.

One area of difficulty lies in the ability to process the information. The pupil has to be able to:

1 scrutinize the problem;
2 find the relevant information;
3 analyse that information;
4 organize it in a logical sequence;
5 calculate the answer to the problem.

The whole process is quite challenging. One misstep and the whole sequence falls apart and you end up with an incorrect answer.

Due to a poor working memory, the pupil with AS will not be able to hold the answer in one part in their head as they proceed to the next step. Therefore they need to be taught how to keep track of the answer as they do each part of the question.

The simple template that follows is designed to help organize the answer because examinations require the sum to be 'worked out' and all the steps put down on paper!

Break it down – example

Salima sees an advert for a summer holiday.

Dates	7 nights	14 nights
1 April – 30 May	£315	£575
31 May – 6 July	£220	£400

Salima books a 7-night holiday in April for two adults. The travel agent adds a percentage surcharge to the cost of the holiday for booking fees. Salima's final bill is £642.60. What was the percentage surcharge?

(AQA Higher Paper 2012)

Number or highlight the stages on the problem

Salima books (1) a 7-night holiday in (2) April for (3) two adults. The travel agent adds a percentage surcharge (4) to the cost of the holiday for booking fees. Salima's final bill is £ 642.60. (5) What was the percentage surcharge?

Transfer each step to the template.

Parts of Question	Calculate	Answer
1. 7 nights 2. in April	Delete 14 nights Delete May – July	£315 per person
3. Total for 2 adults	2 x £315	£630
4. The travel agent adds a percentage surcharge.	The final bill is	£642.60
5. How much is the surcharge?	£642.60 – £630 or $\quad$ 642.60 $-$ 630.00	£12.60
6. What is the percentage surcharge?	12.60 ÷ 630 Simplify: $\dfrac{126}{63}$	2%

Template 14.1 Break It Down

Parts of Question	Calculate	Answer
1.		
2.		
3.		
4.		
5.		
6.		
7.		

World knowledge

World knowledge is the knowledge gained through life experiences, by interaction with one's environment, objects, life events and other people. Research has shown that people with AS have problems processing world knowledge in context and making a judgement as to whether the knowledge is relevant in this context.

Tom is aged 12. While learning about the layout and domestic organization of a wealthy Tudor household, Tom asked, 'Where's the dishwasher?' Ignored at first, he persisted in asking about white goods. He was being serious. Some of the class laughed at him, calling him thick.

The dishwasher is totally out of historical context but the fact that this was a *wealthy* Tudor household might have made it perfectly reasonable for Tom to assume that there would be labour-saving gadgets.

Research suggests that the difference between NT and AS groups when handling world knowledge is probably related to the difficulties the AS group experiences in remembering the exception rather than the rule. This is also evidence of a lack of flexible thinking. Be aware that when learning about a different place or time the pupil may have difficulties adjusting their perspective or thinking to accommodate the differences of a historical or geographical context and the attitudes of those who live in those places and times.

Be prepared for some idiosyncratic conclusions or inferences. Treat them seriously and explain the real differences. Laughing at these gaffs can be humiliating for the pupil.

Reading texts and hyperlexia

Reading skills are important to all subjects. The member of staff who supports a pupil with AS will have to scrutinize the text and anticipate where there will be problems with communication, not just with ambiguity and figures of speech but also with anaphoric cueing (shifting to the use of the pronoun in place of the noun) and historical settings, different places, other countries and cultures.

Be aware of **hyperlexia** – the ability to read words at a level far above what would be expected at the pupil's chronological age. You may also have noticed the inaccurate use of long words in conversation and an odd pronunciation of words. Compliment the pupil for their knowledge and give them the correct meaning. After all, there is nothing wrong with Sesquipedalia (love of long words!) as long as they are used in the right context!

Some pupils with AS will have difficulty identifying and isolating the relevant text when doing a comprehension and seeking the answers. Help them identify key words from the question and use a Reading Blind to focus their attention on the section, that they need to study.

Top Tip

Ask questions of your pupil to check that they have understood what they are reading. This is especially important if it is a literary text because they may struggle with characterization and context.

Reading Blind

A Reading Blind is simply a piece or two of blank, pastel coloured paper to cover the text the pupil is not reading. This helps them focus on the actual text being read.

A more sophisticated Reading Blind is one that doubles up as a place to record notes on the text. See illustration below.

This can be used for any form of writing in any subject but is particularly useful when studying poetry, where an explanation of every figure of speech may need to be noted.

Materials

1 x A3 sheet of blank paper
2 x A4 sheets of paper lined or blank, as required
Sellotape

Use Microsoft Publisher to position text and illustrations, then print onto A3 paper.
  Or

- Print off or photocopy text onto A3 paper in two columns.
- Leave space around the perimeter for diagrams or illustrations, as required.
- Stick two pages of A4 sheets in between the two columns so they can be folded left or right and completely cover the text on either side.
- Fix illustration around perimeter of text.
- Cut the A4 pages into sections to hide some parts of the text but reveal others as necessary: paragraphs, verses, questions... (see Figure 14.2).
- The A4 page on the left covers/reveals the writing in the left column and the A4 page on the right covers/reveals the writing in the right column. See diagram below.
- Use the A4 pages to make notes on the revealed text.
- Photocopy notes onto single sheet for file.

MY LAST DUCHESS FERRARA		Reading Blind
That's my last Duchess painted on the wall, Looking as if she were alive. I call That piece a wonder, now: Frà Pandolf's hands Worked busily a day, and there she stands. Will 't please you sit and look at her? I said	5	Once fixed onto the A3 worksheet to cover all the text, these sheets can be cut to hide sections of the text as required, be it paragraphs or stanzas/lines of poetry.
'Frà Pandolf' by design, for never read Strangers like you that pictured countenance, The depth and passion of its earnest glance, But to myself they turned (since none puts by The curtain I have drawn for you, but I)	10	Two sheets of A4 are needed to cover each side of the paper because
And seemed as they would ask me, if they durst, How such a glance came there; so, not the first Are you to turn and ask thus. Sir, 'twas not Her husband's presence only, called that spot Of joy into the Duchess' cheek: perhaps	15	• the other side of this sheet may be used to write notes relating to the text it covers;
Frà Pandolf chanced to say, 'Her mantle laps 'Over my Lady's wrist too much,' or 'Paint 'Must never hope to reproduce the faint 'Half-flush that dies along her throat'; such stuff Was courtesy, she thought, and cause enough	20	• the text may be laid out differently on the other side;
For calling up that spot of joy. She had A heart- how shall I say?- too soon made glad, Too easily impressed; she liked whate'er She looked on, and her looks went everywhere. Sir, 'twas all one! My favour at her breast, The dropping of the daylight in the West,	25	

Reading Blind

Two sheets are needed to cover each side of the paper because

• the text may be laid out differently on the other side.

• the other side of the sheet from this may be used to write notes relating to the text it covers.

Once fixed on to the A3 worksheet to cover all the text these sheets can be cut to hide sections of the text as appropriate be it paragraphs or stanzas.

Mind your language!

Use oral instruction sparingly: say exactly what you mean and mean exactly what you say.

A pupil with autism will have difficulties understanding all aspects of language – spoken word, tone, intent – and may take everything you say literally. Idiomatic language is particularly problematic. As an exercise to assess the potential difficulties a pupil with AS might face, list the number of idioms and instances of ambiguous language that teachers and TAs unconsciously use while teaching.

A 'simple' instruction, commonly heard in the classroom, 'Write the title and the date in your books' may result in the pupil writing 'The title and the date' rather than 'At Home with the Tudors, 3rd January, 2014' on the page.

Top Tip

DIY instructions, which use as few words as possible, and lots of diagrams are ideal for visual learners.

Difficulties with language

Poor receptive skills and auditory processing

The words they hear may run into each other and get all jumbled up: write down instructions for pupils in a numbered list.

Hyperlexia

They may read words perfectly but not understand them – check comprehension with short questions like: 'What does (this word) mean?'

Visual disturbance and detail focus processing

Large passages of text may be distorted for the pupil or they may only be able to focus on a few words at a time. This also needs to be assessed by asking, 'What does this paragraph tell you about ******?'

If there is a problem, use Reading Blinds to block off the text that is not being read and write explanatory notes on the open blind as described above.

Anaphoric cueing

Check they understand what pronouns refer to. 'Jack rides his bike to school every day. He is never late.' Ask 'Who is he?' and point to 'He' in the sentence.

Literal interpretation

A lack of inhibition may also extend to work done in the classroom. The inability to suppress a literal translation of instructions, together with detailed focus processing, may lead to some very idiosyncratic responses to work set. Clear written instructions broken down to one task at a time, with visual cues if necessary, will be helpful to keep the pupil focused on the task. If this is a major difficulty, speak literally.

Figurative language

Similes and metaphors may need to be translated and the connection or inference (see below) explained in detail because the pupil with AS will be unable to inhibit meaningless comparisons. A good example is taken from Gernsbacher and Robertson's (1999) research: 'Lawyers are sharks.' The intended analogy is that they are aggressive and ferocious, not that they have fins and sharp teeth. The pupil with AS may get an image like this, which is not helpful.

Ask 'Why has (the writer) compared "this" with "that"?' And explain. They will not be able to work out the intention of the author or poet. Use illustrations to show similarities or differences and, in the case of differences, to move on to characteristics rather than visual appearance.

Idioms

Use these in everyday conversation but be sure to check that they are understood and if not, explain the meaning.

Homonyms

These are words that *sound* alike but have different meanings: for example, there/their/ they're; words with double meanings.

Homophones

These are words that *sound* alike and have different meanings, but have different spellings: for example, bough and bow.

Homographs

These are words that are *spelled* the same but have different meanings: for example, fair (colouring), and fair (country festival) and fair (reasonable).

The meaning of these types of words in context may be overlooked and very confusing, especially if words with the same spelling but with different meanings appear close together in a text.

Check comprehension with a simple question about the word as it is used in context.

Inference

This is the conclusion arrived at based upon available evidence. The ability to infer is a complex skill utilizing short term memory if referring to something you have just read or done, such as an experiment in science; long term memory if referring back to a text read or work done in a previous lesson; and world knowledge if referring to information gained from experience. The skill is the ability to judge whether the inference is a reasonable one. In a pupil with AS the cognitive processing required to infer may be disordered. Therefore time must be given to allow for processing.

In order to assess whether the pupil can 'infer', I use simple stories: 'Tim went fishing one morning. When he came home at lunchtime all his clothes were wet. What happened?' Anything that gives a logical reason for this: he fell in the river; it rained; a car drove through a puddle and splashed him; he rescued a dog that fell in the canal... is acceptable.

Or: 'Jack went off to ride his bike for the afternoon. As he turned on to the main road, there was a loud squeal of brakes and a thud. The ambulance arrived to take him to hospital 20 minutes later. Who was taken to hospital?'

When checking for inference skills while reading a text, wait until they have finished reading and allow time for processing.

Questions to ask:
'How do we know that...?'
'Is there any information missing?'

A word of warning – your pupil may not be able to infer when stressed, whereas before they had no problems with inference.

Humour

Jokes may have to be explained. Most pupils with AS seem to love puns and slapstick humour, especially the classics such as Buster Keaton and Harold Lloyd.

Irony, satire and sarcasm

These will have to be explained. Begin with the feeling of the person using these devices and what they hope to achieve.

Echolalia

Repeating what has just been said as an answer. The pupil with AS may not have any other means to answer at the time other than to repeat what you have said. This may be a sign of stress if the pupil does not normally use this method to communicate, as is stuttering and mutism. It may signal overload and shutdown.

Be aware that if you list choices and the pupil repeats the last item on that list, it might not be a selection based upon want or need but simply the repetition of the *last* word.

Non-verbal communication skills

If used, these are likely to be done in an exaggerated manner, as you would find in a cartoon character or a much younger child. The pupil with AS will not be able to read another person's body language or work out a character's state of mind from the description of that character's body language in a text. You will have to explain these and practise decoding facial expressions and gestures, which are the clues to emotions.

Transfer of skills

These may be impaired due to a *lack of flexibility*. A skill such as essay writing in English Language, using PEEL (Point Evidence Explanation Link), taught in one room on a hot, sunny day will not be automatically transferred to the next English lesson, in a different room; or in the same room but on a cold rainy day, or with a different teacher... If this is particularly problematic it is sensible to have a booklet of how to take notes, write a report, sum up an experiment, and so on that the pupil can refer to.

Adherence to rules of grammar and spelling

This is often a strength. Try not to make any errors yourself: they may be pointed out to you in 'that' tone of voice! A pupil with AS is likely to draw attention to errors made because they think that you wouldn't want to make a mistake while teaching. Correct your error – they are invariably right – and thank them for noticing. They are not doing it to humiliate you.

Characterization

Social blindness makes this a particular challenge. A pupil with AS will not be able to infer character from the person's actions or speech. Everything will have to be taught using Personality Plates (see page 120).

Cognitive Empathy or Theory of Mind: placing oneself in another person's shoes

A pupil with autism may believe that you think exactly the same as they do. They are often confused if you tell them your opinion, which is completely different from theirs. Older children may change their answer to match yours, thinking they have made a social mistake. They need to be taught that differences of opinions are acceptable and that their opinion is valid.

Imagination

They have wonderful imaginations and are very creative people – think of the large number of inventors with Asperger Syndrome. What may be lacking is *flexibility*: they may want to do everything their own way or the way they were taught how to do it the first time. You will have to demonstrate good reasons to do it in a different way, such as it being faster or the adult method.

Short sentences and literal language

When issuing instructions, use short sentences and literal language. Word for word, convey meaning without ambiguity. Have visual supports if necessary.

Issuing commands and rhetorical questions v declarative language

Sometimes you may find that commands and rhetoric do not achieve the desired effect. For example: 'Get up now!' Or 'What do you think you're doing down there?' A typical AS response might be 'No!' or 'Lying down!' You could change your approach and make a suggestion as to what they could do instead of lying on the ground. 'If I were you I'd get up now and go to play the game with the rest of your class or Mr Jones will put you in detention.'

Symbol-supported text

If you have a pupil who finds text difficult to process quickly, use Communicate In Print 2 (www.widgit.com) to create symbol-supported text (see below) for worksheets or letters home. At secondary level use this sparingly; every single word does not have to be illustrated.

Say exactly what you mean

Strategies for communication

- Avoid ambiguous language. Think before you speak!
- Use the least number of words you can.
- Do not use a nickname or tease them – they won't appreciate it and may get very upset, not understanding the intention or the emotion behind it.
- To focus the pupil's attention on you, address them by their name first.
- In class the teacher usually writes the title of the day's lesson, the date and learning objectives on the board. Tell your pupil:

    'John, **copy** what Mrs Smith has written on the white board into your book.'

    (It would be helpful if Mrs Smith wrote using a particular colour of ink for the text she wants copied into exercise books.)

- If your pupil has problems focusing on the board, copy a single piece of information, for example Class work, onto an A4 white board and tell your pupil to 'copy the writing on the board' into their book. Rub it off then write the title, for example Adding Fractions. Rub that off then write the date, for example, 1st May, 2014.
- Use the same words for the instruction in each lesson and the pupil will know what to expect and understand what you want them to do. Alternatively, have it written on a piece of paper using symbols (Communicate in Print 2), to which you draw their attention, as and when necessary.
- Pencil an X lightly where you want them to write 'class work', the 'title' and the 'date'.
- If the book is open on two pages and they start to write from the left, be aware that the line continues across to the end of the page on the right. Fold the exercise book over or place a blind (blank piece of paper) on the opposite page so that they only have the page they should write on available to them. Some pupils will be aware of this already.
- Relay verbal instructions: one at a time. *Allow time for processing,* this may differ from pupil to pupil – be patient. Remember to use clear, unambiguous language; do not say, for example, 'Paint the person sitting next to you'. Or you may find another pupil covered in paint!
- Do not repeat the instruction using different words. It will simply confuse them. Choose your words carefully from the outset and repeat the instruction exactly.
- Ask the pupil after the teacher has given an instruction:
  - 'What does Mrs Smith want you to do?'
- Do not say, 'Do you understand?'
- Written instructions are usually presented on a side of A4. This may be too much text. Use the Reading Blind, which is simply a blank piece of paper used to cover up the questions or steps they do not need to concentrate on.
- Do not assume that, after the instruction to open a book at a particular page, the pupil will automatically know to answer the questions on the page or read. Ensure that no part of the instruction process is omitted. Explain each step to them. They will not know what to do unless you tell them.
- Ideally, there should be a school 'house style' regarding the way the page is titled and dated, but I've yet to see this in practice. There may be a department style but, more often than not, each teacher will want it done his or her way. Why can't they all do it the same way? I don't know. Perhaps you could ask the question.
- If the pupil makes a mistake, tell them to put a single line through it. You may find the pupil will want to tear the page out and start again. This may happen at the end of a long piece of writing. Tell them that the 'rule' is to cross out the mistake by putting a neat line through it.

- Always assume they are doing their best. Do not rush the pupil when they are working at a task. They can't go any faster and if you interrupt them at the wrong moment, the house of cards they have so painstakingly built up may all come tumbling down and they will have to start from the beginning again.

Top Tip

Set up a discreet system by which they can tell you when they need help. Traffic signal: red – leave me alone: green – I need help!

Asking the right questions

When supporting a child with an ASC in a lesson never ask:

> How are you getting on?
>
> Do you want my help?

You will get either 'Fine'. Or 'No'.

Very often a pupil with an ASC wants to do the task their way; they cannot tell whether they have difficulties or not; they don't want to draw attention to themselves; they don't want to admit they don't understand.

Observe and ask – 'What do you need help with?' Don't do the work for the pupil!

If strategies to support learning are used, it is likely the pupil will be able to access the curriculum with limited support. However, you should always check.

Some of the common pitfalls are: Can, Could, Would, Should, Will. These are all verbs to avoid in questions because they invite a closed answer (see italics).

Do not say:	**Do say:**
Can you tell me...? *Yes/No.*	Tell me...
Do you know ...? *Yes/No.*	What do you know about...?
Is or Was there a better solution to...? *Yes/No.*	What could he have done differently to effect a better outcome?
Why not write...? Why don't you ...? *They will tell you why not because they think you want to know...*	Give clear instructions. Write...
What happened after...? *May only tell you the thing that happened immediately after*	List the outcomes/results of... Describe four different after-effects ... of ... What were the four effects ...

Find the meaning of...
*May find the meaning but not write it
down or say it aloud.*

and write it down

The following phrases are commonly found in examinations:

Illustrate your answer...
*The pupil may think this means draw
the answer.*

Give examples or
use evidence from the text...

What is the impact of...
What? There isn't one (collision).

Describe the effect of...

Comment on the writer's use of language...
*It's American English because he is
American.*

Use a list or mnemonic as an
aide memoire for everything
that should be included in a
comprehensive response to this
type of question.

Rather than asking an ambiguous question it would be more effective and less confusing to instruct using the following words:

- Tell me... Write down... Show me... List... Explain... Describe... Plan... Use this method to... Design... Build... Compare... Contrast... Investigate... Analyse... Invent... Choose... Recommend...
- Be specific, by using quantity (a specific number) and focus attention on a theme.

Choices

- Choice is particularly difficult for an individual with AS. It may cause distress. Therefore, offer a choice between two things or none at all.
- When offering choices to a pupil with an ASC avoid giving a negative option. Offer two positive options based upon how much you think the pupil will be able to manage.
- Develop this skill with the family – ask them to offer choices and discuss the consequences.
- When the pupil understands that choices have consequences, offer a choice with negative consequences alongside a positive choice to help them make the right choices.

Top Tip

Be consistent and provide clarity and security, giving the pupil self-confidence and enabling them to concentrate on the task. Adjusting to each teacher's different way of doing things is very stressful for an AS pupil.

Top Tip

Teach the pupil to decode examination language in order to produce an appropriate response. Use exam key words from Year 7.

15 Handwriting difficulties, poor working memory and scribing for a pupil with AS

You may find yourself scribing for a pupil on the autism spectrum. Handwriting is a complex skill that we take for granted. The pupil with AS may find it difficult for a number of reasons. Proprioception difficulties and poor fine motor skills may make handwriting awkward due to problems with exerting the correct amount of pressure for the task and forming the letters. Hypermobility and poor muscle tone is also associated with ASCs and they may be unable to hold writing or drawing tools properly. They may also experience pain while attempting to do this.

The working memory is the process by which our brains store information while doing a task. The information is put on standby until needed. A poor working memory means that the information is forgotten, sometimes immediately after the instruction is given. This is very common when the instructions are oral, as typically experienced in classrooms. If the pupil has a poor working memory, difficulties with organizing their thoughts and ideas (planning) and physically writing, the cognitive processing needed to do all these tasks simultaneously makes the whole process very slow, but you will have to be quick to take down what your pupil has said because they will be unlikely to remember and repeat it.

While you are supporting your pupil in class taking notes, or doing any written work for them, it would be advisable to have them dictate the work to you. They will be quite happy to sit back and let you do the work, taking notes directly from the teacher, but in order to engage them in the lesson you will have to ask them to direct you in your note-taking and doing the task set. You can explain that when they sit their examinations the scribe will not be able to write down anything unless dictated by the candidate.

Pupils with AS will need to be taught how to dictate and you need to practise taking dictation with the pupil beforehand because their poor working memory means they may be unable to repeat a sentence that they have literally just spoken. Therefore it becomes even more important that they learn to work with a scribe at a rate where the scribe can write efficiently and accurately. Also don't forget to practise drawing diagrams and graphs. Describing these can be very tricky. They may choose to draw these themselves.

Scribing in examinations

Check the rules of the examination boards. Your pupil will be relying on you to do a good job for them when scribing in examinations and need to be able to trust that you will. The pupil will also be nervous, although they may not appear so, and establishing a rapport with them will enable you to reassure them appropriately.

A scribe needs to be able to:

- Concentrate for a long period of time.
- Remember accurately what the pupil has dictated without having to ask them to repeat themselves.

- Write at speed for a long period of time; the inability to do this will disadvantage the candidate in examinations – practise.
- Write legibly – the pupil as well as the examiner should be able to read your writing.
- And write accurately.

How to scribe for a pupil with AS

1 Arrive in good time to reassure the candidate that you are ready and happy to work for them.
2 Explain to the candidate what you can do as their scribe.
3 Explain to the candidate what you cannot do as their scribe.
4 Be patient. Be quiet. Be still.
5 It may take the candidate with AS some considerable time to read through the question booklet and choose which question they want to answer.
6 Be prepared. Be patient. Be quiet. Be still.
7 It may take the candidate with AS time to organize their thoughts and begin dictating.
8 When they begin to dictate, write down their words as quickly as possible. Due to a poor working memory, they may not be able to recall what they have just dictated to you, so get it down the first time!
9 Let them know when you have finished writing by making an encouraging noise or prearranged signal for them to continue dictating.
10 Ensure they can see what you have written.
11 At the end of the examination congratulate them on a job well done.

Pupils who are likely to need scribes during an examination should be taught how to dictate to a scribe properly as soon as possible, because it is a completely different set of skills.

How to dictate to a scribe

Position

- Sit close enough to your scribe so that you can see what they are writing.
- If the scribe is right-handed: sit to their right hand side.
- If the scribe is left-handed: sit to their left.
- Check that you can read what they are writing.
- Make sure that you are not in the way of their writing.

Speaking to the scribe

- Speak clearly.
- Do not speak too quickly.
- Check that your scribe can write accurately at the speed you dictate.
- Have a bottle of water: you will get thirsty.

Before answering the question, organize yourself

1   Read the question three times.
2   Analyse the question – what do you have to do?
3   Break the question down into sections using subheadings from the key words in the question.
4   Think about what you want to say.
5   Dictate a short plan, a list of key words or notes to remind you what you want to include in your answer/essay.
6   Look at the plan regularly.
7   Delete each point off the plan after you have made it in the essay.

Dictating your essay

1   Use short sentences.
2   Ask your scribe to read aloud what you have dictated to help you think what you want to say next.
3   Need to change anything? Ask your scribe to delete the word, phrase, sentence or paragraph.
4   Continue dictating.
5   Tell your scribe everything you want written down, deleted or moved.
6   Give yourself time to think about what you want to say.
7   Check the time.
8   Diagrams and graphs – you must tell the scribe exactly how to draw these. Give one instruction at a time.
9   Check your work before the end of the examination.
10   Tell the scribe what you want corrected.

When it's all over, scribe, don't forget to praise your pupil for a job well done. And give yourself a pat on the back too. It's very stressful for both of you.

16 Written assignments: be specific

The pupil with AS needs to know exactly what is expected of them. State how many pages, paragraphs or words they are expected to write (depending on the size of the pupil's handwriting if the first two are employed).

For high stakes examination assessments, tell them to aim to write the *maximum* number of words, not the minimum! In my experience, when a teacher tells a class the assignment should be 350–700 words, the AS pupil will stop writing as near to 350 words as they can. They may even stop at 350 words dead, without considering whether they have finished the sentence or not! There may be no shape to the essay. It will simply finish at the word count without development or conclusion.

Or they may continue until they feel that they have finished, with no regard for the time and the fact they have to answer several parts to one question.

As the pupil with AS will be very reluctant to plan their work, it will be of value to give credit for writing a plan. This will encourage them to write one and they need to do this to keep track of the task they are doing. If the plan is part of the required process from the outset, they are likely to plan their work throughout, to their advantage.

Demonstrate the advantages of planning using the appropriate templates.

Worksheets and written instructions

Worksheets are often written in close type with lots of instructions. These are often overwhelming for a pupil with AS. A more effective form of presentation is to break it down to one instruction per page in A5 format.

The following template is designed to clarify the process in the absence of someone to prompt the pupil and is, therefore, an ideal tool for breaking down homework assignments. The initial instruction includes the number of questions or tasks they have to complete overall. At the end of each page is a prompt to proceed from one part of the task to the next.

The sheets are designed to be photocopied back to back, to form an A5 booklet with the centre sheet photocopied as often as needed, depending on the length of the task. Although the sheet is designed to be flexible, I recommend you only write one task per page. The booklet can then be folded over so that the pupil only has to focus on one task at a time.

Don't forget to write down the number of the page if you use the extra sheets, and at the end of the last page.

Template 16.1 Assignment Instructions

Name:...

Subject:...

Class:..

Teacher:..

Assignment/Title:..

....

....

....

....

....

Date set:...

The End.

Well done.

You have now completed your task.

Hand it in to...

Room..

By...

Turn over page.

1

Complete..

Number of words @..................

No less than .... words.

No more than .... words.

Remember to ....

....

....

....

....

....

2

Proceed to page

Proceed to page

Proceed to page

Writing templates

Due to Executive Function Deficit, which is an inability to plan or organize oneself effectively, a pupil with AS may have trouble starting a piece of writing, sustaining a piece of writing and ending it!

There are a number of writing templates in this book, which should not only cover essays for English but other subjects, especially the Factual Essay plan using PEEL.

1 Creative writing.
2 Factual essay plan using PEEL (Point Evidence Explain Link).
3 Argument writing.
4 Compare and/or contras.
5 Conversation.

Most pupils with AS will be reluctant to *plan*, but if ever a pupil needed to do this, it is definitely the individual with AS.

Once the main points have been noted, they can then tick them off as they write (a point per paragraph); this enables them to see their progress while developing a sustained piece of writing.

Begin with the template with link words to provide clear direction before moving onto the blank template.

Creative writing

You will have to focus the pupil's attention on what is required using the creative writing template. This is based on the development of a story, not the number of paragraphs.

Use the boxes to outline the story:

1 Set the scene.	WHERE?
2 Introduce the characters.	WHO?
3 Create the problem or challenge.	WHAT AND WHY?
Include dialogue.	*WHO SAYS WHAT TO WHOM?*
4 Describe the struggle.	HOW?
5 The climax.	SUCCESS or FAILURE

This is very loosely based on the beginning, middle and end format but with more guidance for development of character.

Drawing stick figures in the first column reinforces both the story scenario and the idea provides an illustration of the progression of a story.

Develop their skills by focusing on a step at a time:

1 Set the **scene**.	Descriptive detail reflecting the mood
2 Introduce the **characters**.	Describe 1 or 2 of the people
Include dialogue.	Conversation or argument
	(avoid 'said')
3 What is the **conflict?** Why?	Action (avoid 'went')
4 How? Describe the **struggle**.	Descriptive detail – action
5 The climax.	Resolution – action, reflection

Top Tip

Find out what sort of story the pupils are going to be asked to write about and have a selection of pictures for the pupil to refer to that illustrate the scene, characters and some of the action.

For example, a ghost story may have a couple of figures walking in a wood at night, and an adventure story may involve people stranded on some rocks as the tide comes in. Use the pupil's interest as a starting point, if appropriate. A science fiction fan may be interested in writing a story set in space; fantasy in another world; a train journey on the Orient Express. Do not give more that two choices.

Template 16.2 Creative Writing

Title:..

....

Where? Scene	
Who? Characters	
What happens? **How?** **Why?** **The Plot** **The Conflict**	
The CLIMAX! **The END**	

Factual essay writing

By including the levels attained for completing each part, the pupil with AS will see what he/she will gain (literally) from writing in this style. Write the levels at Key Stage 3 in the headline of the template thus:

POINT Level 3	EVIDENCE Level 4/5	EXPLAIN Level 5/6	LINK Level 7

The template can be used to prepare for essays in most subjects about any topic.

- Teach the pupil to read the question carefully and decode language.
- They should be encouraged to identify and highlight the key words, which tell them what they have to do.
- Check that they have understood the question by asking the following questions:
  - What is the title directing you to do?
  - How are you going to do this?
  - What is your opinion of the...?
- Pay particular attention to the opening/introductory paragraph of the essay. I recommend that the pupil extracts words from the title to discuss in general terms.
- Because pupils with AS have difficulty placing themselves in another person's shoes, they may be under the impression that you and everyone else think the same as they do. Validate their opinion, providing they can back it up with good reasons.

Template 16.3 Factual Essay

Title/Question:..

....

POINT	EVIDENCE	EXPLAIN	LINK

Inference

Inference may be confusing to a pupil with AS. They are being asked to look at the evidence and refer to their world knowledge, make a connection between the two and come to a conclusion based upon the information given. The evidence to support the conclusion is in the form of a clue in the text rather than an actual statement. The pupil needs to be taught how to read 'between the lines'.

John left the house carrying his bucket and spade.
Where is he going? To the beach.
How do you know this? What is the clue to the inference he is going to the beach?
He is carrying his bucket and spade.

John left the house carrying his   bucket and spade.

Top Tip

Use the magnifying glass symbol to alert the pupil that when reading this passage and answering questions on it, they have to search for clues and make inferences from the text.

If you ask the question: 'What do you infer from this passage?' the most likely response will be a repeat of the action described.

Differentiated Inference templates

1 Copy the TEXT being analysed into the Inference template 16.4 into the column: 'I read this'.
2 Write down the FACTS into the second column: 'I know that'.
3 Write down the CLUES into the third column: 'The clue is'.
4 Write down the INFERENCE into the fourth column: 'I conclude that:'.

Use Inference template 2 when you want to develop the skill of reading the text and predicting what is going to happen next.

Use Inference template 3 when you are confident they no longer need written prompts.

Start teaching inference by giving the answers and asking the pupil to find the inferred evidence to support this. Use different colours as shown below.

Inference Exercise

1 Read the following passage.
2 Put a circle round the clues.

"John, go down to the shop and buy a bottle of milk, please," his mother asked as she handed him her purse.

John went into the hall and pulled on his coat and woolly hat. He sat on the stairs to pull on his wellies. Then out he went, slamming the door behind him. She watched his hunched figure stomping off down the road.

Fifteen minutes later he returned, marched straight into the kitchen and put the milk down on the table with a thump, glowering at her as he returned to the hall.

3 Where are the clues that tell you:
a) John and his mother have run out of milk.
b) It is cold outside.
c) It is wet outside.
d) John doesn't want to go.
e) John feels cross.
f) John is angry with his mother.

You should get something like this. However, don't be surprised if the pupil doesn't realize that 'she' refers to John's mother and 'he' to John. Some pupils have difficulties with anaphoric cueing.

"John, *go down to the shop and buy a bottle of milk*, please," his mother asked as she handed him her purse.

John went into the hall and *pulled on his coat and woolly hat*. He sat on the stairs to *pull on his wellies*. Then out he went, *slamming the door* behind him. She watched *his hunched figure stomping off* down the road.

Fifteen minutes later he returned, *marched straight into the kitchen and put the milk down on the table with a thump, glowering at her* as he returned to the hall.

Template 16.4 Inference 1

I read the text below:	I know these FACTS: !!	The CLUE is:	I conclude the INFERENCE is:

Inference 2 – I Predict

I read:	I know these FACTS !!	The CLUES are	I predict that this will happen:

Inference 3

TEXT	FACTS !!	CLUES	INFERENCE

Writing to argue, inform, persuade and advise

You cannot assume that the pupil with AS will infer from the information given who the audience is or the correct style of writing they should adopt.

The first template of 16.5 is used to focus the pupil's attention on this decision. The simple mnemonic GAPS is to remind them what they should take into consideration:

- Genre (type of writing, for example story, report, analysis)
- Audience (who are you writing for?)
- Purpose (why are you writing this?)
- Style (what style or form should it take in order to serve the purpose and appeal to the intended audience?)

This can be used in any subject.

Initially, the pupil should be given a list of publications and/or scenarios with the correct style of writing beside each, which they can refer to.

The inability to be flexible means that they may have to learn the list by heart.

There are three Writing templates, which may be used to prepare for a discursive style of writing:

- Two points of view (with link words and phrases)
- Compare and contrast
- Speech bubbles
- Boxes and bubbles

The Conversations templates are designed to be flexible in order to support a number of tasks.

Two points of view

This template gives the pupil a high scaffold with the link words and phrases. With the conjunctions or connectives (words used to connect ideas and evidence) it provides a model of how the writer moves fluently from one idea to the next and should be used if the pupil is uncertain how to link ideas and paragraphs in the 'arguing to persuade' element of the English Language examination. As they become more competent, move on to the template without the connectives and prompt the pupil to use their own words.

Compare and contrast

This template may be used for any topic in any subject where the pupil has to consider two objects, ideas, characters, times, countries or two points of view. Animal or vegetable? 50s or 60s? Hot or cold lunches? Catholic or Protestant? Boy thinks this and Girl thinks that? Hitler and Chamberlain? You and me? Anything!

The template is designed to show a clear separation of ideas to help organize their thinking and make the writing process easier.

The speech bubbles

These can also be used to develop the writing of dialogue in an English essay or to plan the progress of a conversation in Modern Foreign Languages in preparation for the oral element of the assessment.

This template may also be used to conduct a basic Comic Conversation – questions and answer.

And the final Conversations template has boxes in between the speech bubbles for agreement and disagreement or giving two people's different points of view on the same subject.

Top Tip

It is also worth noting that different writing styles are used in different subjects and an awareness of the appropriate style of writing for each subject will benefit the pupil.

Template 16.5 GAPS – Genre, Audience, Purpose and Style

Essay Title:	
Key Words:	
Genre – the type of text I will be writing is: (a letter, newspaper article, speech, information leaflet, advertisement) Because:	
Audience – the people who are going to read this are:	
Purpose – I am writing this to:	
Style – therefore, I will write in a friendly/formal/ humorous...	Style.
Writing devices I will use are: (rhetorical question, repetition – power of three, personal experience, statistics, facts, opinion, plea)	
Vocabulary – words I shall use	

Argument Writing – 2 Points of View

INTRODUCTION The question of.../ the idea that is....

This may be true

It is often said …

This argument does not convince me…

Nevertheless,

It has been suggested…

I am convinced that…

However,

Opponents of … say that…

I disagree with this because…

Alternatively,

Advocates of this... say...

In spite of that, I …

To sum up... Finally... Therefore, I would argue that...

Compare and Contrast

17 English Literature

Literature can be particularly difficult for pupils with AS because of their lack of social awareness and inability to place themselves in another person's shoes. They are often visual learners; some have excellent memories for dialogue and can quote large chunks of films they have seen. Observe your target pupil and try and identify how they learn best. It may be more effective for them to have illustrated texts.

There are a number of ways you can access this genre:

Use graphic novels and plays rather than plain text

I can recommend John McDonald's Shakespeare plays and *Frankenstein and Dracula* by Jason Cobley, who has also produced a graphic play of *An Inspector Calls*. McDonald's Shakespeare plays are differentiated to three levels – original text, plain English and shortened versions. They are also supported with interactive motion comics using celebrated Shakespearean actors, available at: www.classicalcomics.com

Watch the film of the play or novel

An authentic portrayal of the play in its proper context is best. Luhrmann's *Romeo and Juliet* with its modern context will be very confusing. Use Zeffirelli's version.

A word of caution: nudity and violence can be distressing for an individual on the spectrum. Speak to the parent. Warn the pupil before watching the film.

YouTube

This is a good resource for poetry readings and films made about poetry used at GCSE. For example: morrismovies has a little gem in its cartoon-graphic portrayal of 'Dulce et Decorum Est' by Wilfred Owen.

Filming a poem

Either in an animated version or acting out the scenario, this is a good way of exploring the comprehension of the pupil with AS and developing it. 'My Last Duchess' by Robert Browning and other monologues or poems with voices are very accessible.

PowerPoint handouts

With one or two lines of poetry per slide, illustrated with relevant images, three slides to a page with lines for jotting down notes, these are very effective in enabling observations to be referenced to the appropriate lines in the text.

Create a booklet

Creating one's own booklet of challenging poetry should also be considered.

Visual references are very helpful in establishing the context, be it historical, geographical or social. A glossary of relevant terms and dictionary can also be incorporated as notes into the booklet for immediate reference and provide a strong scaffold to support learning and understanding. Granted it is a lot of work initially but, once done, is available to generations of pupils.

Colour coding the text to highlight imagery: metaphor, simile and symbol, characterization, theme or any aspect of the text you want to focus on may also be helpful.

Colour is a very powerful tool – always use the same colour to illustrate the type of text you want to reinforce. Using blue for metaphor in one poem and then red to highlight metaphor in another poem is not helpful – be consistent.

Background notes on the writer's inspiration, the historical context and the literary form of the text may be added to provide world knowledge cueing for the pupil before reading the text. Add no more information than is necessary to support understanding of the text. A pupil with AS may take the historical context of the text to mean that the poem or novel is fact not fiction.

Design the booklet to have the poem and notes on the left hand side of the booklet with the illustrations on the right and the relevant line beneath as a reference to the text.

Note: Wikipedia is a good source of information and illustrations to support the study of historical poems.

Reading blinds

Use reading blinds to focus on the part of the poem being studied by covering up the rest of the text. The blank centre paper may also be used to write notes relevant to the text.

Visual references

Pupils with AS are visual learners. It is, therefore very helpful to have visual references relating to the text. Alternatively, you can illustrate a text by drawing a scene, using stick figures. I drew scenes from *Of Mice and Men* by John Steinbeck on A3 sized paper. Stick figures may be made easily recognizable as the characters through the use of simple, visual references, symbols and colours, which represent physical characteristics or personality traits. No need to draw faces.

For example: Lenny was very large, square head and fingered hands (the other characters only had a single line for a hand); Crooks' angle in his back, his head was coloured in; Candy bent over and a hand missing; and George was small with a hat...

This illustration is devised to support the understanding of relationships and dialogue and therefore uses speech bubbles. The pupil identified and selected the appropriate quotations from the text and transcribed them onto the cartoon.

Illustrations

Another format to support teaching poetry is to divide A3 paper into 6 sections for illustrations, with a space beneath the picture for one to two lines of a poem (see below). Another space for notes or a reference to the relevant text may also be accommodated in the design.

I am no artist, as you can see! What is important is that the text is represented by the inclusion of the objects in the poem: cloak and gloves. The illustrations are made by tracing the figures from Renaissance portraits using pencil, then charcoal to darken the cartoon. I photocopied the characters and repositioned them to reflect the action in the poem. The portrait I used here to illustrate Browning's Porphyria's Lover is 'Wounded Man (self portrait)' by Gustave Courbet (1819–1877) from the Musée d'Orsay.

Figure 17.1

Figure 17.2
Based upon Young Girl Fixing Her Hair by Sophie Anderson from Wikimedia Commons – a free resource.

The pupil should copy out the lines of poetry beneath the relevant illustration.

Films

When watching films, be aware that dramatic licence may be accepted as a true representation of the text.

Top Tip

Use original text audio books or recordings because some individuals with AS have an excellent memory for film dialogue and/or audio recordings.

Sam, aged 16, was a film buff. He was able to remember the action and dialogue of films verbatim. Sinise's (1992) film of the novel *Of Mice and Men* is not totally accurate and whenever the novel was mentioned Sam quoted verbatim the one scene in the film that doesn't appear in the novel. My telling him to forget that scene was ineffective. In the end I read the novel out loud to him during revision lessons.

Top Tip

Type 'Graphic novels/plays' into the search engine of an online book shop and you will find a large number of illustrated texts, from popular stories for children to novels by the Brontë sisters.

Resources

Shakespeare, W. (1606/2008). *Macbeth – The Graphic Novel: Original Text*. Unabridged. John McDonald (Adapter), Karen Wenborn (Collaborator), Nigel Dobbyn (Colourist), Jo Wheeler (Designer), Clive Bryant (Editor), Jon Haward (Illustrator), Gary Erskine (Illustrator). Classical Comics; British English edition.

Shelley, M. (1818/2008). *Frankenstein – The Graphic Novel: Original Text.* Jason Cobley (Adapter), Karen Wenborn (Collaborator), Jon Haward (Collaborator), Jason Cardy and Kat Nicholson (Colourists), Jenny Placentino (Compiler), Jo Wheeler (Designer), Clive Bryant (Editor), Declan Shalvey (Illustrator), Terry Wiley (Illustrator). Classical Comics; British English edition.

Personality Plates

There are two Character Templates. 'Plate' 1 in Template 17.1 has a single 'face'.

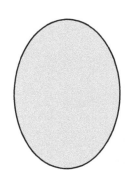

Draw the character on the oval shape using symbolic features: a caricature. Draw visual references next to the personality profile; for example, Curley's wife = big eyes looking upwards, large eyelashes (see Figure 17.2); Curley angry = narrow eyes looking right out at you, v-shaped eyebrows. List aspects of the character's personality with a suitable quotation under evidence, and add page references.

The drawings do not have to be great, just enough to get the idea across.

The template is designed to draw attention to the need to note a number of personality facts and the textual evidence for them. Too often the AS pupil will give a single reason in response to a question because that is all he has been asked for. Until examination boards enumerate the number of comments they require, the AS pupil will have to be taught to give as many different reasons as he can think of.

Template 17.2, Comparing Characters, has two 'heads' but can also be used for discussing historical characters, or morphed into animals. Items can be drawn or stuck into the middle of the oval. They are designed to be flexible.

The two-headed template is also a good tool to use when teaching Social Skills or Cognitive Empathy exercises to enable the pupil to see that while he thinks one thing based upon what happened, another person might have a completely different viewpoint.

Template 17.1

Character's name:..

Personality Fact

is...

....

....

....

....

....

....

....

....

....

....

Evidence

because...

....

....

....

....

....

....

....

....

....

....

Template 17.2 Comparing Characters

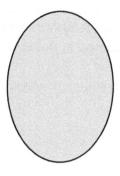

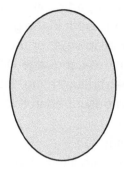

Name...

Fact..

Evidence...

....

F...

Ev...

....

F...

Ev...

....

F...

Ev...

....

F...

Ev...

Name...

....F

....Ev

....

....F

....Ev

....

....F

....Ev

....

....F

....Ev

....

....F

....Ev

Poetry

Poetry presents particular challenges for the pupil with AS because it is a highly sophisticated use of language both in the grammatical and creative sense. Original metaphors and similes will cause major problems for them and each one will have to be explained in detail, as discussed in the chapter on Language Difficulties.

I recommend illustrating the poem and you can do this in a variety of ways, which have already been described in this book:

- PowerPoint
- Workbook with illustrations
- Cartoon
- Work mat with illustrations.

Creating a work mat on A3 paper is a very effective tool. The poem goes in two columns in the centre of the sheet, surrounded by images relating to the content, with the double page reading blind affixed to the centre for making notes on the poem directly opposite the relevant lines.

Poetry analysis – step by step

The mnemonic is a useful device when supporting the inclusion of a number of elements in a complex task for someone with a poor working memory. CATS DIRRT FO, which lists what the pupil has to do in an in-depth study of a poem, is one such, and well laid out is a good guide for someone to write a comprehensive response to the unseen poem.

- **Content** – summary of what the poem is about.
- **Aim** – the intention of the poet.
- **Theme** – the idea of the poem and the poet's feelings about it.
- **Syntax** – the positioning of the words in a sentence and their relationship to each other.
- **Diction** – the poet's choice or use of words to express meaning.
- **Imagery** – figures of speech in writing, literature, etc., that produce a specified effect, mental images.
  - **Illustrated Imagery:** I have added another page to the section on imagery with boxes for pictures of the poet's images. The first box should contain a literal interpretation of the image, for example 'she was as graceful as a swan' should have a picture of a swan in the Picture box and in the Meaning box a picture of a graceful woman. You will have to explain the connection.
- **Rhythm** – a regular arrangement of sounds, and of stressed and unstressed syllables, giving a sense or feeling of movement; metre is the arrangement of words and syllables, or feet, in a rhythmic pattern according to their length and stress; a particular pattern or scheme, for example Iambic pentameter = ' / or di dah.
- **Rhyme** – a pattern of words that have the same final sounds at the ends of lines in a poem. A Rhyme Scheme is plotted using a letter of the alphabet to identify each rhyme sound. Begin with the letter a, then b and so on. I have plotted the rhyme scheme for the first stanza of 'Charge of the Light Brigade' by Alfred, Lord Tennyson below. If you underline the lines in a different colour corresponding to the letter, it helps you to establish at a glance whether or not there is a pattern in the rhyme.

• Half a league, half a league,	a
• *Half a league onward,*	b
• **All in the valley of Death**	c
• *Rode the six hundred:*	b
• 'Forward, the Light Brigade!	d
• Charge for the guns' he said:	d
• **Into the valley of Death**	c
• *Rode the six hundred.*	b

- It is worth noting that some poems are identified by their rhyme scheme, for example a limerick: aabba, abbaab; a Petrarchan sonnet: abbaabba, cdecde; and a Shakespearean sonnet: ababcdcdefefgg.
- **Tone** – a quality or character of the voice expressing a particular feeling or mood.
- **Form** – structure and organization in a piece of writing, the outward appearance, if appropriate: a calligram, for example, is a poem formatted in the shape of a picture. Certain types of poems have a specific number of lines, for example a limerick has five, a sonnet has 14.
- **Opinion** – write what you think of the poem and explain why.

This may also be the basis for an eleven-paragraph essay, one step at a time, using the notes made in the template.

Top Tip

In order to demonstrate how a poem should be read – to the punctuation, not the end of the line – read it with the pupil, taking turns by alternately changing over at each punctuation mark.
Read the poem aloud to your target pupil, exaggerating the emotions of the text.

Template 17.3

POEM TITLE: .... POET ....

TYPE of POEM: ....

TASK	EXAMPLE	QUOTATIONS	COMMENTS
Content A summary – What is the poem about?			
Allusion – reference to other literature?			
Aim – poet's intention. Why is the poet writing about this?			
Good story, interesting character, sharing an experience...			

TASK	EXAMPLE	QUOTATIONS	COMMENTS
Theme: what is the main idea? Love, jealousy, time passing, nature, religion, death.			
Syntax: the order of the words in the lines. Fluent sentences, clumsy grammar Slang or Dialect. Voice – a way of speech peculiar to the persona (a monologue) or the poet's 'voice'?			

TASK	EXAMPLE	QUOTATIONS	COMMENTS
Diction contd: alliteration – repetition of consonant sounds;			
assonance – repetition of vowel sounds;			
onomatopoeia – word sounds like the sound it describes;			
sibilance – sss,			
caesura – pause mid line,			
enjambment – idea goes from one line/ stanza to another without pause.			

TASK	EXAMPLE	QUOTATIONS	COMMENTS
Imagery: Simile (cue like/as);			
Metaphor			
Personification – inanimate object given human characteristics – the wind screamed in fury. Pathetic fallacy: human feelings given to nature – smiling sun, cruel wind			

TASK	PICTURE		QUOTATIONS	COMMENTS
	Image	Meaning		
Insert or draw a picture of the image into the EXAMPLE box.				
(Imagery includes the following:				
Simile,				
Metaphor,				
Personification				
Pathetic fallacy)				

TASK	EXAMPLE	QUOTATIONS	COMMENTS
Rhythm: movement, meter: arrangement of words & syllables, or feet, in a rhythmic pattern according to their length and stress; a particular pattern or scheme. Iambic Pentameter? Does it sound like the subject? Does it change during the poem?			
Rhyme: pattern in the sound at the end of the line – eg rhyming couplets aa bb, Alternate rhyme scheme abab? English Sonnet: abab, cdcd, efef, gg or Italian Sonnet abba abba cddcdd, cdecde?			

TASK	EXAMPLE	QUOTATIONS	COMMENTS
Tone – Atmosphere and Mood: Humorous, Ironic Sad, Melancholic Romantic, Tragic Eerie, Mysterious Insane, Dark Any other…			
Form – outward appearance: structure and organization. How many lines to a stanza (verse)? Effect of it shape Ballad, calligram, limerick, sonnet?			
Opinion: I think the poem is… because…			

18 GCSE Drama project

When embarking on a GCSE Drama Project, which entails numerous different tasks undertaken over several weeks, the instruction sheet can be very daunting for a pupil with AS.

The following worksheets or workbook breaks the project down into manageable tasks for the pupil to work through a page at a time. Notes should be made on the worksheet to be word processed later in the format required by the examination board.

Note that space has been provided for diagrams or symbols illustrating the text to support comprehension of the task.

Top Tip

Have the pupil illustrate the template, highlighting key terms with a symbol in the box under the sub-heading.

Support them to ensure they understand exactly what is required and in their choice of an appropriate symbol as a visual prompt.

Template 18.1 GCSE Drama Project Notes

Use full sentences – not bullet points

(1) Response

Stimulus: (play, physical theatre, document, newspaper article, photo)

Group Response to the Stimulus:
(What ideas did you have because of the stimulus?
Think outside of the box be creative.
List 3–4 different things.
This stimulus made my group think of:

1)

2)

3)

4)

My Response: This stimulus made me think of

It is different from the other stimuli because

(2) Strategies I might use to Explore My Response:

Techniques		Effects
Thought tracking		
Flashback		
Cross-cutting		
Mime		

Techniques		Effects
Still Image		
Slow Motion		
Monologue		
Asides		
Narration		

(3) Development

Storyboard – Use ...... boxes below to draw the key moments of the plot.

<u>Writing in Role</u>

Write a diary entry or a letter as if you were the person you are 'acting':

<u>Symbolism</u>

(things used to represent ideas eg a clock for time, clothes for a type of character or a job)

By using

we intended to make the audience think about:

Extract from the dramatic response piece

Characters:

Scene:

Action:

How I used Stanislavsky's ideas of Super Objective:

When in the hot seat I was asked about:

<u>What do I</u> (as the character) <u>do?</u> **I replied**:

<u>Why do I</u> (as the character) <u>do it?</u> **I replied**:

<u>How do I</u> (as the character) <u>do it?</u> **I replied**:

<u>My character's super objective</u> (**overall aim** in the drama) is:

I show the super objective of my character by:

I used the following **actions** and **gestures** to help me develop my character's feelings

I created my character by:

I showed my character when I used:

Dialogue	by
Accent	by
Body Language	by
Use of voice	by
Gestures	by
Tension and Suspense	(See next page for tension graph) by
Twist in the Tale (an unexpected ending)	by
Levels	by
Costume	(see separate page for drawing)

10																				
9																				
8																				
7																				
6																				
5																				
4																				
3																				
2																				
1																				
0																				
L A B E L S																				

Proxemics, Communication, Status, Character and Relationships

Draw a labelled diagram of the 'stage' showing how space was used to show:

The character's status (position in society/family)

Relationship with other characters.

Costume

Draw the costume in detail, in the space below. Colour it in.

Explain why you chose the fabric/colour/shape to suit your character.

Colour:

Fabric:

Shape:

It suits my character because

Lighting, Sound Effects and Props

We used the following **lighting effects** to:

We used the following **sound effects** to:

We used the following **props** to:

We changed the following effects:

because

because

because

because

(4) Evaluation

Stimulus – the stimulus made us think of:

Strategies – explain how dramatic techniques helped the audience to understand the plot and made it more interesting:

Character – my character was made clear to the audience by:

In **rehearsal** I changed: (explain why you made these changes)

Voice – I used my voice to (explain what you were trying to do and how you did it)

Movement – I used movement to (explain what you were trying to do and how you did it)

Lighting – the lighting we used was effective because:

Sound – the music and sound effects were effective because:

Props – the props we used were effective because:

Costume – my choice of costume was effective because:

Set – Describe your set and explain your choices and changes. Our choice of set was effective because:

My performance – I was **good** at:

I could have **improved**:

OVERALL – I thought I was **strong** at:

I **communicated** the message:

to the audience.

(5) EVALUATION OF THE OTHER GROUP'S WORK:

What did they do well?

What could have been done **better** and **why**?

If I could **redo** this project I would **change**: (state your reasons)

19 Interpreting images: English Language, History and Geography

In many subjects the pupil will have to be able to discriminate between images that give different information. Pupils with AS may have difficulties with time, place, fact and fiction, and they can be very confused when given images to comment on. They should be taught how to interpret visual images, especially those used in high stakes examinations.

Establishing a *consistent* method for doing this in every subject is helpful.

Strategy

They should be encouraged to:

1 read the question;
2 underline the key words;
3 study the picture in detail;
4 then look at the picture as a whole.

Begin from a certain point on the image. This could be the central focal point of the image – the person or feature – before focusing on details that they are naturally inclined to 'see'. Use a coloured pen to draw the circle of focus and ask the questions (see below).

End with the whole image and the general impression it gives, which is important to the interpretation of the situation to be discussed.

In English Language they may have to discriminate between images being used to inform and those used for advertisement purposes, to persuade. Teach the difference, including the language of colour. Red as a symbol of danger and anger is obvious; other colours do not have such strong associations with abstract ideas or emotions and will have to be taught.

In History a painting or a photograph may present an idealized portrait or a satirical representation of a character or an event. Cartoons are often used, and the tendency to interpret words and images literally can lead to confusion.

In Geography the images are usually 'stating the obvious', but the pupil may be captured by the detail, not the whole picture.

Interpreting Images Exercise (1)

Teach the pupil a method of scrutinizing the image using the following questions:

1 Who or what is portrayed in the image?
2 What kind of image is it?
   - Explain that a painting is likely to be an idealized portrait or a representation of an event.
   - A cartoon is usually humorous and/or satirical. See Interpreting Cartoons, below.
3 Where/when did this event take place?
4 Look at the background – what do you see? Are there any other people in the picture? What are they doing?
5 Look at the centre/focal point of the picture – what do you see?
6 What is the attitude of the main character? Look at his body. Is he calm and triumphant? Is he tired and cold?
7 Are there any things in the painting that look out of time and place?
8 Is the picture an idealized portrait? Is it realistic? Is it fantastic? Is it humorous? Is it sarcastic?
9 Are there any symbols or details reinforcing the message in the picture?
10 What conclusions do you come to, when interpreting images?

Place an overhead projector film transparency over the image. Using different coloured dry wipe pens, jot down the questions below one at a time. Using the same colour, circle that part of the image you want the pupil to focus on to answer the question. Ask the pupil to copy the question and answer on paper. Wipe the plastic clean and go on to the next question. Always us the same colour for the question whenever you repeat this type of exercise.

The Questions

Who?   Red

What is s/he doing?   Blue

Where?   Green

Other people?   Orange

What are they doing?   Black

Why are they doing this?   Yellow

How do they feel?   Purple

'Napoleon Crossing the Alps'

Delaroche, St James' Palace

David Levine, 1964
Reproduced by kind permission of Matthew Levine

Interpreting Images Exercise (2)

Compare these two images of 'Napoleon Crossing the Alps' with 'Napoleon Crossing the Alps on 20th May, 1800' by Jacques-Louis David and 'Napoleon doing a Wheelie', which can be found on Google Images.

Tell the pupil to study the four images carefully, one at a time. Ask the pupil to describe each image with one of the following labels:

1 Ideal
2 Humorous
3 Fantasy
4 Realistic

...and then to justify their choice:

- Why is this image an ideal portrait?
- What makes this image funny?
- Why is this image fantasy?
- Why do you think this is the most realistic portrait?

They may not see Napoleon crossing the Alps on a motorbike as 'fantastic'. Go through each image one at a time and discuss the portrayal of Napoleon.

Top Tip

Practise, practise, practise using images from past papers in English Language, History and Geography. Be *consistent*. Once you have established a method, use it with the pupil across the curriculum subjects.

Interpreting Cartoons

Cartoons are found in every History GCSE paper. Each cartoon has the following characteristics:

- humorous, usually in a satirical tone;
- image is exaggerated – caricature of well-known figures;
- informative – about a specific event;
- focal point;
- use of symbols;
- caption – a title or brief explanation of the picture;
- expresses an opinion of the artist or publication, which may reflect the national feeling.

The picture is usually made up of people and objects that have special significance to the *message* of the cartoon.

There will not be anything in the cartoon that does not contribute to this message.

Template 19.1 Cartoon Analysis

Picture	
	Audience:
	People in Cartoon:
	Objects in Cartoon:
	Symbols & Meaning:
	Action:
	What is the message of the cartoon?

Words								
Cartoon Caption:	Key word/s:	Emotions:	Dates and their significance:	What event is the cartoon referring to?	What led up to this event?	What took place after this event?	Explain the significance of the cartoon:	

Timeline

The 'Timeline' is a simple but very effective tool that is often overlooked. It is also one that pupils can easily draw for themselves and that brings order to the task.

Its potential uses are:

- to plot Dates
- as a Development Tracker, for example volcanic eruption, plant growth, events leading to …
- Time Management – cooking
- any plan that requires the pupil to be aware of 'time'.

To make a timeline take a rule and draw a line down the left hand side of the page or across the bottom of the page; for example this 2-hour timeline for a cookery lesson with 10, 30, and 60 minute 'lines'.

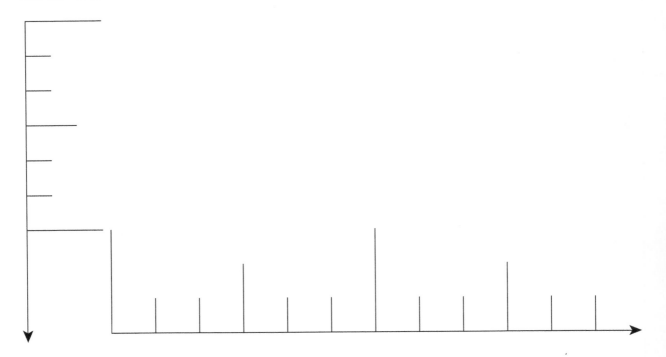

Maps

Maps are useful tools when working with an AS pupil, as 'place' in the context of the lesson may have little meaning for them. It would also be useful to have the distance north to south or east to west noted, with a scale of distance. Remember that abstract concepts may be difficult ideas to grasp for a pupil with an ASC.

You may need to draw the Brandt line (north-south divide between countries highlighted by their socio-economic wealth or poverty, devised in the 1980s); highlight specific countries and climate in Geography; or draw the Maginot Line (French fortifications built before World War 2 along the border with Germany in the 1930s) in History.

While supporting a pupil in the study of the Literature from Other Cultures module, a set of maps is useful to have in English, especially when studying poetry by foreign poets. I found myself using a map of North America in several English lessons to show where events in *Of Mice and Men* took place.

Carry a folder of maps. I had copies of the British Isles, World, Europe, Asia, Australia and New Zealand, North America and South America. You never know when you might need them, and not just for the lesson. I have also used them to play guess the country or capital city... to distract a pupil.

Website

http://www.freeusandworldmaps.com/html/WorldRegions/WorldRegionsPrint.html

20 Practical subjects: Science and the Technologies

Pupils with an ASC have a number of difficulties that may impact on their conduct and learning in these subjects, on top of language difficulties and understanding instructions.

Cognitive processing

- Pupils may have problems hypothesizing and predicting before conducting an experiment or making something.
- Detailed focus processing may mean that they focus on a part and do not get the bigger picture.
- Conversely, DFP may also mean that they will be able to see the detail and pick up mistakes or data others miss.
- Perfection: the need for perfection may inhibit their rate of progress or even attempting a task they don't feel confident about.

Literacy

- A whole new vocabulary needs to be learned and what may mean one thing in everyday language may mean another in Science or Technology, for example, tissue meaning a group of cells combining as the material that organisms are made of, or thin paper for wrapping or absorbent paper.

Sensory

- Pupils may have sensory difficulties dealing with practical subjects.
- Hypersensitive senses can result in an extreme reaction; for example, a hypersensitive sense of smell can lead to the pupil being sick in a science lesson. Or a hypersensitive sense of touch may mean the pupil cannot handle food or paints. Forcing a pupil with these hypersensitivities may lead to the pupil becoming distressed. However, you may find that the pupil enjoys the sensations on offer and covers their hand in paint or flour; or obsessively strokes a cloth and hammers wood.
- Hyposensitivity may cause issues regarding health and safety; for example if the pupil is less sensitive to touch they may burn themselves.

Poor motor skills

- May mean that the practical subjects are more difficult.
- Proprioception and vestibular difficulties may make the pupil clumsy when walking round the practical area.
- Handling equipment may be awkward and accidents are more likely to happen.
- Using unfamiliar tools and utensils may cause the pupil pain.
- Measuring exact amounts of a substance, such as pouring water into a jug or a beaker, may be difficult.

Organization

There is a large amount of organization needed to prepare for and carry out the experiments or produce the practical work in Science and Technology. The array of equipment, tools and utensils are likely to be confusing, especially if there are different tools that do similar jobs. The pupil with ASCs may find it difficult to:
- make a decision
- know how to start
- sustain a piece of work
- and how to finish it.

Rigid behaviour

This may result in the following:

- A lack of understanding that tools and equipment have multiple uses.
- An expectation that they will use exactly the same tools each lesson.
- A rigid interpretation of the rules may mean that if they are told not to touch something – they won't, ever. They are likely to adhere to the rules of the lab or tech room to the letter.
- A difficult relationship with peers who 'bend' the rules.

Harry's Year 8 science class had been told always to wear goggles and stand up when doing an experiment. The class was reminded of this at the beginning of each practical lesson. He checked everyone was obeying the rules. If he found someone without their goggles or sitting on a stool, Harry would reprimand them and tell the teacher. He had to work alone until his TA found a group of peers who would tolerate his behaviour and help him focus on the experiment by giving him specific jobs to do.

Health and Safety

Many people have concerns regarding the ability of pupils with ASCs in practical lessons for the following reasons:

- Meltdowns in practical lessons.
- Sensory issues may make wearing safety equipment, like goggles, intolerable.

- A pupil with an ASC may not be aware of the dangers of some procedures, equipment or materials being handled.

Strategies

Cognitive Processing

- A hypothesis is a statement that can be tested, for example, plants need light to grow.
- Formalise it using the following:
  - **If I do** ... (explain what you are going to do – grow a plant in a dark place) **then** ... (this **will happen** – it won't grow).
- Break down tasks using templates.
- Complete task one step at a time.
- Allow time for processing.
- Support with illustrations and diagrams.

Literacy

- Make up key words list for each topic, with illustrations or symbols.
- Use a science dictionary.

Sensory

- Check the pupil profile for any sensory issues.
- Make reasonable adjustments: allow them to wear ear defenders in metal work, woodwork and music lessons and plastic gloves in Food Technology when handling food.
- If the practical lesson is likely to be a major difficulty that the pupil clearly cannot handle, then the pupil can be given the job of record keeper.

Motor skills

- A TA should be assigned to support a pupil in any practical lesson if there are difficulties with motor skills, in order to fetch the necessary tools and equipment. This will minimize the pupil's travel about a room or provide a helping hand when needed. Please note, the pupil may not ask for help – be alert.
- Keep all the equipment needed to complete the task in a high-sided, plastic tray on the work area. Have this prepared before the start of the lesson or give the pupil the tray with an illustrated list of equipment they need to collect.
- If necessary, use equipment specially adjusted for weak grip and hypermobility. The pupil may experience pain using the equipment for any length of time.

Organization

Some pupils will not need such a high level of support.

- Use a key fob for pre-lesson preparation as necessary. Get out:
  - Text books
  - Exercise books
  - Pencil case
  - School Planner
  - Put bag away... (on shelf, under bench)
  - Put on Lab coat, goggles, gloves...
- Place all equipment needed for the lesson into a deep-sided plastic tray.
- Or use an illustrated list for gathering the equipment needed for the task into a deep-sided tray. (A key fob of the different pieces needed can be made up before the lesson.)
- Include illustrated instructions for the practical task, with visual references (diagrams of tools or science equipment).
- Keep the text to a minimum. Word-free DIY instructions are the best for a pupil with an ASC.
- The instructions should include a diagram or photograph of the correct, final set-up of the equipment or finished product.
- Remember that, in some situations or with some pupils, you should only progress one step at a time, that is, one step on one piece of paper.
- Practical subjects end with the tidying up process – a list of what to do to clean up properly and where to put things away would also be helpful. Colour coding equipment and their storage areas will take a lot of time at the outset but save time later for all students.
- Hazards of conducting the practical task should also be highlighted, using illustrations.

Rigid behaviour

- Demonstrate all the practical uses of the equipment.
- Some pupils may get upset if someone else is using 'their' equipment. Make a note of the equipment they have used and, if possible, use the same tools. You might be able to overcome this by getting them to use different pieces or have a workstation dedicated to all pupils with rigid behaviour with a set of tools assigned to that workstation.
- Refer them to the instructions on how they will complete the task in each lesson.
- Put together a group to work with the pupil, who know of, and are tolerant and understanding of, their behaviour.

Health and Safety

- Do not assume that the pupil will be able to infer from the task set what the hazards are.
- Make sure the pupil understands the labels alerting users to the type of hazard the material presents.
- Place a laminated, illustrated list of the hazards associated with the task into the equipment tray.
- Ask the pupil to tell you what are the hazards of doing the task.

Science

Some of the world's greatest scientists have Asperger Syndrome and it is often one of the areas of strength for a pupil on the autism spectrum because it deals with facts and figures. The great scientists went on developing their area of interest until they became super-specialists and, never giving up, made some discoveries that have, quite literally, changed the world. However, many scientists did not show this promise in school.

Learning the facts of science subjects may be relatively easy – it all being logical and governed by natural laws. There are several areas of difficulty you need to be aware of:

- **Cognitive processing:** hypothesizing and predicting before conducting an experiment.
- **Sensory issues** with the smell of labs and chemicals, clothing and safety equipment.
- In **Biology** the human body and especially anything to do with sexual reproduction may cause distress for some pupils. They find it all too horrible to contemplate...
- **Planning and organization** when conducting an experiment.
- **Lack of flexible thinking and transfer of skills:** in a different room or conducting a different experiment the pupil may need to be taught how to use a piece of equipment they have used before.
- **Poor fine motor skills:** the pupil may not have the ability to measure precise amounts of water into a beaker or test-tube without assistance.
- **Poor gross motor skills:** the pupil may be clumsy moving about the classroom.
- **Hazards**, something that may cause harm, will include the following:
  - Fire – gas rings, electric rings, oven, iron, glue gun, Bunsen burners...
  - Electricity – circuits, faulty wiring, damaged plugs or sockets...
  - Chemicals – acids and alcohol...
  - Micro-organisms – bacteria...
  - Glass...

  This is not an exhaustive list – check with the subject teacher.
- Here is a link to a little game that will alert the pupil to the hazards of a science lab: http://www.interactivesolutions.co.uk/games/flashGames/labHazards.htm
- **Bullying:** the reaction some pupils with an ASC have to certain science topics and NT pupils' banter surrounding certain terms, such as vibrator, may show up the AS pupil's ignorance or distaste. This can lead to that pupil being tormented and taunted publicly with their ignorance or clear distress at something they consider to be revolting or which should be kept private.

Strategies

1 Use the following templates to support the pupil in science experiments: Investigative Skills Assignments (ISA) Booklet, and Practical Subjects.
2 Apply the strategies outlined above.
3 Divide the data collection box (page 8 of the ISA Booklet) into the required number of sections needed for the experiment.
4 Collect any graph data on a separate sheet of paper and staple the completed graph into the booklet when it has been completed.
5 If the pupil has proprioception difficulties, or hypermobility, you may have to record the data for them. Treat this as if it were an exam: use a sharp pencil to record the data.
6 Page 9 has been left blank for any diagram results such as you might find in biology and culture growth.

Investigative Skills Assignments (ISA) Booklet

Name: ....

Form: ....

Subject: ....

Date: ....

Teacher: ....

Room: ....

Teacher's Comments

What you did well: ....

....

....

....

....

How to improve: ....

....

....

....

Evaluation

Consider: Equipment and Method and Explain why...

I could have improved upon my experiment by:

....

....

....

....

....

....

....

....

....

Hypothesizing

A hypothesis is an idea I have about something based upon what I can sense (see, hear, smell, taste or feel).

I need to conduct an experiment to gather evidence to prove that my idea is correct.

Statement: ....

....

....

....

Therefore, if I ....

....

then ....

.... will happen.

Diagram Results

Equipment List

Observations

1.

Method

1.

Diagram

Risk Assessment

Hazard: ....

Risk: ....

Control ....

Data

	1	2	3	4

My Experiment

I want to find out...

....

I am going to...

....

INDEPENDENT VARIABLE – change:

....

DEPENDENT VARIABLE – measure:

....

CONTROL VARIABLE – remains the same:

....

Conclusions

I found that...

....

....

....

My hypothesis was/wasn't backed up by the results because:

....

....

....

....

Technology – Woodwork, Metalwork, Textiles and Food and Art

The need for perfection may make practical subjects difficult for the pupil to carry out. They may become fixated on getting it absolutely right or, if they make a mistake, want to throw it away and start again.

While most of the aforementioned strategies may be applied to these subjects, they come with a different set of issues regarding health and safety.

- Ensure that you have the information to relay the dangers of the equipment used (with diagrams) in the equipment tray.
- Whenever there are mechanical tools involved, especially electric tools, do not simply rely on diagrams to convey safety information.
- Ask the teacher to take the time to demonstrate how to use such tools properly, highlighting the hazards as they do.
- Most workrooms have 'instructions for safe use' on a sign next to the relevant machinery; ensure that this is supplemented with diagrams. It would be helpful to show the risks in a diagram too.
- Make sure that the pupil has a list of materials needed stapled into their school planner, homework diary, or Comms Book – they may lose it or forget to inform their parents that they need to bring in materials for a lesson.
- Use the Practical Subjects template to focus their attention on what needs to be done.

Template 20.2 Practical Subjects

Subject: ....

Task: I have to ....

....

....

I need: (Equipment) ....

....

....

....

....

....

I am going to: (Method) ....

....

....

....

....

....

....

....

At the end of the lesson I need to: ....

....

....

....

21   School trips

School trips are great opportunities to expand life experiences and to develop life skills. Good organization and planning is the key to any successful school trip and if pupils with AS are in the group, they will need to be carefully organized too. Anxiety will be the overwhelming emotion – the fear of the unknown and the lack of control.

Once a letter home has been sent, contact the parents to check that they have received it and invite them into school to discuss the trip and how best you can help prepare the pupil together. Some pupils may be well travelled and need the minimum support.

Discuss travel experience and modes of transport they are familiar with. What are their daily routines for getting up in the morning and going to bed at night, relaxation techniques, food, sensory issues, phobias, use of public conveniences, sharing a room?

The pupil's family may have tried and tested travel routines and be able to give advice on any potential difficulties.

Wherever possible, apply routines already used by parents and keep everything as predictable as possible. If there are strategies used by parents to reduce anxiety levels – audio or games devices, puzzle books or sketch or note pads – use them.

Can they be given their own room? This will help greatly with the need to have their own space and time to unwind. Taking their own duvet and pillow may help them settle.

The level of differentiation depends on how competent and/or how anxious the pupil is. The main thing is to ensure that the pupil with AS feels safe and knows what to expect. The level of scaffolding may be reduced after negotiation if you feel the pupil is managing the trip well.

Strategies before the trip

- Assign the key TA to the pupil several weeks in advance to prepare for the trip.
- If the key TA can also accompany the pupil on the trip to help monitor and manage the child, this would be ideal. A trusted member of staff, whom the pupil knows will be there to help at all times, will relieve the stress.
- The key TA to discuss with the pupil what they need to know, what is likely to cause stress and how to alleviate it.
- Familiarization – special attention must be paid to any new experiences. If the pupil has never been away from home before it would be useful for their parents to give them the experience of sharing a room, and visit a hotel.
- Long distance travel on a coach and managing service stations during stopovers to use the toilets or get a snack can be practised.
- It may be the first time the pupil has ever flown or gone on a ferry. They need to be told what to expect when they reach the airport/ferry terminal and on the aircraft/ferry. If the airport/ferry terminal is nearby, it may be helpful for the parents to take them on a preliminary visit.

- Create a School Trip booklet with the pupil. Include space for a diary and recording anything to do with their special interest that they may find on the trip: birds and insects, foreign number plates and makes of cars, postcards and stamps.
- A list of things to pack for a residential trip and any special equipment needed should be sent home. It is also a good idea to ask the parents to have a checklist of all the pupil's belongings on a spreadsheet so that they can keep track of them if they are staying in several different locations.
- Have the pupil pack a daysack or small bag to carry during the journey, with copies of travel documents and other papers in a plastic, zipped envelope, wallet/purse, snack, drink, books, puzzles, audio or games devices to help distract them.
- Outline what to do in an emergency, such as locking themselves out of the hotel room. Write a list of concise instructions to help the pupil feel more secure.
- Assign a couple of carefully selected buddies to support the pupil. Check they are acceptable to the pupil.
- Food may cause difficulties due to sensory issues. Discuss this with the parents. Generally speaking, basic foods such as plain meat and potatoes, pizza and pasta will be acceptable. Rules should be clear and concise. Explain what behaviour you expect and why. These may also be written down.
- Describe and discuss the physical signs of distress the pupil might feel when anxious. Give the pupil strategies to monitor these and how to calm themselves and at what point help should be sought.
- Discreet signals should also be arranged for the pupil to indicate levels of stress to staff members or trusted buddies who know them well.
- When taking the pupil through the programme, discuss and agree what to do should the pupil become anxious. This is especially important if a TA is not specifically assigned to support the pupil throughout the day.
- Exchange mobile phone numbers and ensure enough credit for the trip is on the pupil's phone.
- Check instructions for the dispensing of any medication.
- Agree a time to contact parents. The pupil may need to speak to parents every day or intermittently. If the latter, be aware that the parents will also be anxious and would appreciate a call from you to reassure them all is well.

Maps are useful visual aids

- When using a single map for the whole trip, trace arrowed routes in different colours for different days.
- Itinerary – supplement the map with a timeline including dates, times and places, using as few words as possible.
- Approximate times may be helpful. Use the term: ETD (estimated time of departure) 0900 – 0930 and ETA (estimated time of arrival). Potential for delay should be explained. Use an analogue clock with the approximate time shaded.
- Use illustrations of key sites, e.g. airports, ferry terminals, hotel, tourist sights, ruins, museums.
- For a daily itinerary use numbered dots to indicate the order the sites will be visited, with different colours for mornings and afternoons. Directional arrows may be helpful.
- Include maps of large sites and a pre-arranged meeting point, rendezvous times.

Strategies during the trip

- Arrive at the departure point before the pupil so that you are there to greet them and distract them should there be any delay.
- Retain original documents and give out spending money as needed for the day. Poor organizational skills may result in the pupil losing passport, tickets and money. Have different purses for different currencies.
- Documents in their daysack should include an autism alert card (translated into the language of the country being visited or travelled through), staff name and mobile telephone number, school telephone number, name of the travel company. These should be self-explanatory to the authorities because, faced with a crisis, the pupil may not be able to communicate effectively.
- Do not deviate from arrangements agreed with the pupil unless you have discussed and agreed any change beforehand.
- Monitor mood and reactions carefully but don't be overly fussy. If you have done your preparation well, then the pupil will know what to do in any eventuality.
- If you want to develop the pupil's independence, arrange to meet at regular intervals at pre-arranged rendezvous points throughout the day.
- Use the mobile phone to set alarms as reminders. An accompanying note on the appointments calendar will help remind the pupil where, when, who...
- Do not make food an issue by drawing attention to any idiosyncrasies associated with it. Respect the pupil's choice even if it is exactly the same at each meal each day. The need for sameness may be the need for predictability and security.
- Unstructured leisure time may be difficult for the pupil. Do not force them to go to participate in a sporting event or to a disco. They will need time to recharge after a day of new experiences. They may prefer to fill in their trip diary or simply be alone for a time playing on a portable gaming device.
- Enjoy the trip and the new perspective your pupil with AS will give you!

Resources

A light-hearted film is *First Time Flying Documentary* by Jamie Davey on YouTube, (not suitable for younger children): http://www.youtube.com/watch?v=2Zf85y4hmXo

Afterword

So we have come to the end. I hope that it will be a beginning for you. I set out writing this book because I saw that many of us needed to understand why we had to make these accommodations for the pupil with an ASC or Asperger Syndrome.

Autism is a hidden disability and because of this a large number of autistic pupils are finding themselves failed by the mainstream education system. The numbers in alternative educational provision like Pupil Referral Units are rising in some areas of the country because some schools are not willing to learn how to manage these children. Due to government standards, their eyes are firmly fixed on examination results and, while they are prepared to pay for any amount of training to raise results, some are reluctant to invest in the 'small' number of pupils who, ironically, with support could actually produce good academic results.

These pupils need your understanding, tolerance and all the support you can give them to be accepted and respected for who they are; to survive in school, develop skills and achieve so that they can have a rewarding future and contribute to society, as is their right.

It is my hope that you will take the ideas in this book and develop your own strategies and methods to support your own individual Asperkids in accessing the curriculum and joining in the communal life of the school. They want to do well and be a part of it all – they just don't know how.

Accept   Respect   Protect

Glossary

Definitions of autism spectrum conditions are taken from the National Autistic Society webpage: http://www.autism.org.uk/About-autism/All-about-diagnosis/Jargon-buster/Glossary-of-terms-a.aspx

Other definitions are mostly taken from the online *Oxford Dictionary of British English* (http://oxforddictionaries.com).

ABC chart chart used to analyse incidents to effect better outcomes in future.
- **A**ntecedent – what happened leading up to the problem behaviour;
- **B**ehaviour – the observed problem behaviour;
- **C**onsequence – the event, which immediately follows the response.

affective empathy able to feel physically what others are feeling.

alliteration the occurrence of the same letter or sound at the beginning of adjacent or closely connected words (e.g. big blue balloon).

allusion an expression designed to call something to mind without mentioning it explicitly; an indirect or passing reference.

amygdala a roughly almond-shaped mass of grey matter inside each cerebral hemisphere, involved with the experiencing of emotions.

anaphoric cueing using the pronoun to refer to the noun that precedes it.

aside a remark or passage in a play that is intended to be heard by the audience but is supposed to be unheard by the other characters in the play.

Asperger Syndrome (AS) an autism spectrum condition that affects the way a person communicates and relates to others. A number of traits of autism are common to Asperger Syndrome including:
- difficulty in communicating
- difficulty in social relationships
- a lack of imagination and creative play.

However, people with Asperger Syndrome usually have fewer problems with language than those with autism, often speaking fluently though their words can sometimes sound formal or stilted. People with Asperger Syndrome also do not have the accompanying learning disabilities often associated with autism; in fact, people with Asperger Syndrome are often of average or above average intelligence. NAS

Asperkid an affectionate term for a child with Asperger Syndrome.

assonance resemblance of sound between syllables of nearby words, arising particularly from the rhyming of two or more stressed vowels, but not consonants (e.g. how now brown cow), but also from the use of identical consonants with different vowels (e.g. killed, cold, culled).

AS Unit special unit in school designed to meet the needs of pupils with Asperger Syndrome; or Autism Spectrum Unit.

auditory or aural sense of hearing.

Autism spectrum condition (ASC) a broad range of lifelong, neurological and physiological conditions, which affect the way people behave and interact with the world socially, sensorially, in their use of language and a lack of flexibility.

Autism on its own is also known as **Kanner's Syndrome/Classic autism** or **Low Functioning Autism (LFA)** a lifelong developmental disability that affects the way a person communicates and relates to people around them. Children and adults with autism are unable to relate to others in a meaningful way. Their ability to develop friendships is impaired, as is their capacity to understand other people's feelings. All people with autism have impairments in social interactions, social communication and imagination. This is referred to as the triad of impairments. NAS

AutOS Autistic Operating System; as in Mac OSX computer operating system, the way the OS runs the programs.

avoidance behaviour avoidance by people with autism of the everyday demands made by other people, due to their high anxiety levels when they feel that they are not in control. NAS

backhanded bullying where a pupil with AS is misled to do something inappropriate, thereby getting them into trouble.

Bombmeter a 0–10 emotional assessment tool in the shape of a thermometer with the spectrum rising to red.

caesura in poetry, a pause near the middle of a line.

CATS DIRRT FO mnemonic to remember what to include in poetry analysis.

cerebral hemisphere each of the two parts of the cerebrum (left and right) in the brain of a vertebrate: the left hemisphere plays a dominant role in the comprehension of language.

cerebrum the part of the brain located in the front area of the skull and consisting of two hemispheres, left and right, separated by a fissure. It is responsible for the integration of complex sensory and neural functions and the initiation and coordination of voluntary activity in the body.

cognitive empathy being able to understand how others are feeling, without feeling the emotion themselves.

Comic Conversations devised by Carol Gray, comic strip conversations are visual representations of the different levels of communication that happen in a conversation. NAS

compare and contrast compare: similarities; contrast: differences.

cross cutting two or more scenes of a play that are performed on stage at the same time.

declarative language describes what it wants to accomplish rather than focusing on how to achieve that goal.

dendrite in *Physiology* a short-branched extension of a nerve cell, along which impulses received from other cells at synapses are transmitted to the cell body.

detail focus processing to focus on details while disregarding the whole.

dialect a particular form of a language, which is peculiar to a specific region or social group.

dialogue a conversation between two or more people as a feature of a book, play, or film.

diction the choice and use of words and phrases in speech or writing.

differentiation presenting educational material to pupils in different formats and methods in order to enable them to make sense of it and process it so they can learn effectively, regardless of differences in ability and learning styles.

DSM-IV *Diagnostic and Statistical Manual of Mental Disorders*, the American Psychiatric Association's (APA) diagnostic reference book, now replaced (May 2013) by DSM 5.

Dyslexia disorders that involve difficulty in learning to read or interpret words, letters, and other symbols, but that do not affect general intelligence.

Dyspraxia impairment or immaturity of the organization of movement with associated problems of language, perception and thought. NAS

echolalia repetition of another person's spoken words as a means of communication in autism.

egocentric thinking only of oneself, without regard for the feelings or desires of others.

enjambement in poetry, the continuation of a sentence without a pause beyond the end of a line, couplet, or stanza.

Executive Function the ability to plan and carry out complex cognitive tasks. In autism this ability is interfered with by dysfunction in the frontal lobes of the brain (Trevarthen *et al.*, *Children with Autism*). NAS. EF deficit includes a poor working memory, inattention, and difficulties initiating, sustaining and inhibiting actions.

Executive Functioning Skills organizational skills.

exit card a small card given to pupils with special needs. The pupil shows it to the teacher when they have to leave the lesson.

figurative language departing from a literal use of words.

fine motor skills these use the smaller muscles and are used to pick up and manipulate small objects, to write and to fasten clothing.

flashback a scene in the past before the current action in the play.

flash forward a scene in the future after the action in a play.

fMRI scans functional magnetic resonance imaging scans, which detect blood flow through the brain and is used to measure the brain's response to stimuli in experiments conducted to find out how the brain operates.

form the visible shape or configuration of a poem.

frontal cerebral cortex the outer layer of the cerebrum (the cerebral cortex) at the front of the brain, composed of folded grey matter and playing an important role in consciousness.

frontal lobe each of the paired lobes of the brain lying immediately behind the forehead, including areas concerned with behaviour, learning, personality and voluntary movement.

GAPS in factual essay writing, consider Genre (type of writing), Audience, Purpose and Style of writing.

glycine amino acid that is present in blood platelets and serum, which acts as a neurotransmitter.

graphic novel/play novels and plays in cartoon form.

grey matter the darker tissue of the brain and spinal cord, consisting mainly of nerve cell bodies and branching dendrites.

Gross Motor Skills these use the larger muscles and are used to walk, jump, run and general movement in sports.

gustatory sense of taste.

heterogeneous diverse in character; in autism this means that no two people share the same characteristics, therefore each person with autism presents differently with the condition.

High Stakes Examinations examinations that impact upon your future studies and career choices.

hippocampus the centre of emotion, memory, and the unconscious nervous system.

homographs words that are *spelled* the same but have different meanings.

homonyms words that *sound* alike but have different meanings; words with double meanings.

homophones words that *sound* alike and have different meanings, but have different spellings.

hot seating in Drama, a character is questioned by the group about his or her background, behaviour and motivation.

hyperbole exaggeration.

hyperlexia being able to read (from a very early age in some cases) without really understanding what you have read.

hypermobility particularly supple and able to move their limbs into positions others find impossible. They may have a degree of low muscle tone and suffer from joint pain, back pain and be prone to dislocated joints and soft tissue injuries.

hypersensitive having an extreme physical sensitivity to particular substances or conditions.

hyposensitive having a reduced sensitivity to particular substances or conditions.

hypothalamus a region of the forebrain that coordinates both the involuntary or unconscious nervous system and the activity controlling body temperature, thirst, hunger and involved in sleep and emotional activity.

iambic pentameter in poetry, rhythm shown by 5 metric feet, di dah (short long) -/-/-/-/-/.

ICD-10 World Health Organization's *International Classification of Diseases*. The European reference book for medical professionals to consult when making a diagnosis.

idiom an expression of a given language that is peculiar to itself grammatically or cannot be understood from the individual meanings of its elements.

idiomatic language the language we use every day, rich in local expressions and sayings.

idiosyncratic behaviour strange behaviour peculiar to the individual.

imagery visually descriptive or figurative language, especially in a literary work.

inference the conclusion arrived at based upon available evidence.

Inset Day In Service Training Day for school staff.

interpreting images what does the photograph tell the viewer about the person/place/time? Commonly found in English Language, History and Geography.

intervention action taken to improve a situation.

irony the expression of one's meaning by using language that normally signifies the opposite, typically for humorous or emphatic effect.

Kanner Syndrome/classic autism neural developmental disorder characterized by impaired social interaction and verbal and non-verbal communication, and by restricted, repetitive or stereotyped behaviour. The diagnostic criteria require symptoms to be apparent before a child is three years old.

key fob laminated aide memoires on a key ring to remind the pupil what to do in any given situation. Colour code to task.

Key Stages ages at which a pupil is expected to achieve a certain academic standard.

key words the words associated with a topic being studied, or the words in an essay title or question, that tell the reader exactly what they have to do.

Learning Support Assistant (LSA) aka teaching assistant.

Learning Support Centre where the SEN Department are based as a subject, to meet the needs of the pupils on the SEN register.

literal interpretation taking words in their usual or most basic sense without metaphor or exaggeration; words that do not deviate from their defined meaning.

litotes understatement.

LSA Learning Support Assistant aka TA or teaching assistant.

meltdown an uncontrolled emotional outburst, which is a neurological response to stress or sensory overload.

metaphor a figure of speech in which a word or phrase is applied to an object or action to which it is not literally applicable (e.g. he is a lion).

metre a unit of measurement or the rhythm of a poem.

mime the theatrical technique of suggesting action, character, or emotion without words, using only gesture, expression and movement.

mnemonic a system such as a pattern of letters, ideas, or associations that assists in remembering something.

monologue (dramatic monologue) a poem in the form of a speech or narrative by an imagined person, in which the speaker inadvertently reveals aspects of their character while describing a particular situation or series of events.

myelin a whitish insulating sheath around many nerve fibres, which increases the speed at which impulses are conducted.

narration a character tells the story.

NAS National Autistic Society: UK charity for people with autism.

neural relating to a nerve or the nervous system; patterns of nerve activity.

neuron a specialized cell transmitting nerve impulses; a nerve cell.

neuro-physiological disorder a condition brought about by natural differences in the formation of the brain that cause difficulties in processing.

neurotransmitter a chemical substance that is released at the end of a nerve fibre by the arrival of a nerve impulse and, by diffusing across the synapse or junction, effects the transfer of the impulse to another nerve fibre, a muscle fibre, or some other structure.

Neuro Typical (NT) term coined by the autistic community to refer to those not on the autism spectrum.

olfactory sense of smell.

onomatopoeia the formation of a word from a sound associated with what is named (e.g. cuckoo, sizzle).

opinion a view or judgement formed about something, not necessarily based on fact or knowledge.

pathetic fallacy the attribution of human feelings and responses to inanimate things or animals, especially in art and literature.

pathological demand avoidance an autism spectrum disorder where individuals resist and avoid the ordinary demands of life, using skilful strategies that are socially manipulative (distracting adults, using excuses, appearing to become physically incapacitated) (Worthington, A. (ed.), *Fulton special education digest*). NAS

PEEL (Point Evidence Explanation Link) method for focusing pupils' attention on the content of factual or critical essay writing in response to a question for coursework or examination.

peer intervention action taken with peers of the pupils with AS to improve a situation or the relationship between them.

persona (plural: personae) the main character in a poem.

personification the attribution of a personal nature or human characteristics to something non-human, or the representation of an abstract quality in human form. A figure intended to represent an abstract quality.

pervasive developmental disorder not otherwise specified (PDD-NOS) disorders that fit the general description for pervasive developmental disorders, but in which contradictory findings or lack of adequate information mean that the criteria for other pervasive developmental disorders cannot be met. (ICD10). NAS

pica a tendency to eat substances other than normal food.

proprioception sense of movement and the awareness of the body in space – position.

proxemics the amount of space that people feel it necessary to set between themselves and others, which in Drama shows the relationships between characters.

psychiatry the study and treatment of mental illness, emotional disturbance and abnormal behaviour.

psychology the scientific study of the human mind and its functions, especially those affecting behaviour in a given context. An Educational Psychologist specializes in the context of education.

pun a joke exploiting the different possible meanings of a word or the fact that there are words that sound alike but have different meanings.

Pupil Passport document outlining information about the individual, useful to all school staff.

Pupil Referral Unit local authority establishment that provides education for children unable to attend a mainstream school.

Retts Syndrome a profoundly disabling neurological disorder that only affects girls. A slowing of development and regression, with loss of skills in speech and hand use and social withdrawal, that begins at around one to three years. Motor development is severely impaired, with difficulty in planning and coordinating movement. NAS

rhetoric the art of effective or persuasive speaking or writing, especially the exploitation of figures of speech and other compositional techniques.

rhetorical question asked in order to produce an effect or to make a statement rather than to elicit information.

rhyme correspondence of sound between words or the endings of words, especially when these are used at the ends of lines of poetry.

rhythm the measured flow of words and phrases in verse or prose as determined by the relation of long and short or stressed and unstressed syllables.

role stepping into another character's shoes.

role model someone the pupil with AS can identify with and admire.

sarcasm the use of irony to mock or convey contempt.

satire the use of humour, irony, exaggeration, or ridicule to expose and criticize people's stupidity or vices, particularly in the context of contemporary politics and other topical issues.

savant a person with a learning disability who has pool(s) of extraordinary ability.

scribe to write for the pupil.

SEN register list of pupils in the school with a Special Educational Need.

SENCo Special Educational Needs Co-ordinator: head of the SEN Department in school.

Sensory Box a (shoe) box with items used to stimulate or soothe the senses.

Sensory Break time out from the school 'day' to either calm down or stimulate a sense.

Sensory Integration Disorder (SID) or Sensory Processing Disorder (SPD) a condition present in autism, but also separate from it, by which the senses are disordered resulting in hypersensitivity and/or hyposensitivity to the seven senses: vision, hearing, touching, smell, taste, balance and movement.

sensory overload the sensation becomes unbearable and the brain shuts down or goes into meltdown.

sensory room a room filled with sensory tools to soothe or alert the senses for the pupil who needs a sensory snack during a sensory break.

sensory snack an activity done in the sensory break to soothe or alert the senses.

sequipedalia – love of long words like hippopotomonstrosesquipedaliophobia, which means a fear of long words!

serotonin a compound present in blood platelets and serum, which acts as a neurotransmitter.

shutdown where the body shuts down and the individual is unable to respond due to overload or stress.

sibilance a hissing sound.

simile a figure of speech comparing one thing with another thing of a different kind, to make a description more emphatic or vivid; using the word like or as (e.g. as brave as a lion).

slang a type of language consisting of words and phrases that are regarded as very informal, are more common in speech than writing, and are typically restricted to a particular context or group of people.

social stories used to teach social skills to people with autism. Devised by Carol Gray, they are short descriptions of a particular situation, event or activity, which include specific information about what to expect in that situation and why. NAS

spectrum a wide range.

Stanislavsky (System) intense character development process that strives to make a performance 'real' and not artificial. In order to achieve this realism, the system is used to:
- Bring an actor's experiences into the role
- Expand an actor's imagination.

stanza a verse in poetry.

still image individuals or groups to invent body-shapes or postures, rather than freeze existing action.

stim stim (verb) is short for indulging in self-stimulatory behaviours, or (noun) a stimulatory behaviour.

stimulus a thing that arouses interest, activity or energy in someone or something; a spur or incentive.

storyboard a sequence of drawings, typically with some directions and dialogue, representing the scenes planned for a play.

strategy a plan of action designed to achieve a long-term or overall aim.

super objective main theme of the play.

symbol (a) a thing that represents or stands for something else, especially a material object representing something abstract. (b) A mark or character used as a conventional representation of an object, function, or process, e.g. the letter or letters standing for a chemical element or a character in musical notation.

symbolism (a) the use of symbols to represent ideas or qualities. (b) An artistic and poetic movement or style using symbolic images and indirect suggestion to express mystical ideas, emotions and states of mind.

synapse a junction between two nerve cells, consisting of a minute gap across which impulses pass by diffusion of a neurotransmitter.

syntax the arrangement of words and phrases to create well-formed sentences in a language.

TA – Teaching Assistant aka LSA or Learning Support Assistant.

tactile sense of touch.

tension graph graph used to plot the tension in a play or text.

theme an idea that recurs in or pervades a work of art or literature.

Theory of Mind (ToM) a philosophical concept of the understanding one has that another person has an individual perspective on states of affairs, that this consciousness depends in part on information that they may have which is not available to oneself and vice versa (Trevarthen *et al. Children with autism*). NAS

thought tracking the group makes a still image and individuals are invited to speak their thoughts or feelings aloud.

timeline a line representing a period of time, on which important events are marked.

tone the general character or attitude/mood of a place, piece of writing, situation.

Tourette syndrome – characterized by multiple tics characteristically involving the facial area (twitches, blinking, nodding) as well as phonic (vocal) tics. The onset of symptoms usually occurs between the ages of 2 and 21. NAS

transition moving from one place to another: primary to secondary school or lesson in room 1 to lesson in room 7.

vestibular sense of balance.

voice the attitude of the character as revealed by what they say or in the case of poetry – what the poet writes.

white matter the paler tissue of the brain and spinal cord, consisting mainly of nerve fibres with their myelin sheaths.

workmat A3 paper with key words, symbols and pictures to illustrate the content of the lesson.

world knowledge the knowledge gained through life experiences of interaction with one's environment, objects, life events and other people.

Bibliography

A Cognitive Defense of Stimming (or Why "Quiet Hands" Makes Math Harder) http://musingsofanaspie. com/2013/06/18/a-cognitive-defense-of-stimming-or-why-quiet-hands-makes-math-harder/ Retrieved from the Internet, 13 July 2013.

Ambitious About Autism, Stats and Facts retrieved on 16 December 2013 from: www.ambitiousaboutautism. org.uk/page/about_autism/stats_and_facts/index.cfm

APA (1994). *Diagnostic and Statistical Manual of Mental Disorders*. Fourth Edition (DSM IV). Washington, DC: American Psychiatric Association.

AQA Mathematics Higher Paper, Number, London, 2012.

Attwood, T. (2006). *The Complete Guide to Asperger Syndrome*. London: Jessica Kingsley Publishers.

Barnard, J., Prior, A. and Potter, D. (2001). *Inclusion and Autism: Is it working?* London: The National Autistic Society.

Baron-Cohen, S. (2008). *Autism and Asperger Syndrome: The facts*. Oxford: Oxford University Press.

Beeman, M.J. and Bowden, E.M. (2000). Right and left hemispherical cooperation for drawing predictive and coherent inferences during normal story comprehension. *Brain and Language*, 71, 310–336.

Bogdashina, O. (2005). *Communication Issues in Autism and Asperger Syndrome: Do we speak the same language?* London: Jessica Kingsley Publishers.

—— (2006). *Theory of Mind and the Triad of Perspectives on Autism and Asperger Syndrome: A view from the bridge*. London: Jessica Kingsley Publishers.

—— (2010). *Autism and the Edges of the Known World: Sensitivities, language and constructed reality*. London: Jessica Kingsley Publishers.

Church, C., Alisanski, S. and Amanullah, S. (2000). The social, behavioral, and academic experience of children with Asperger Syndrome. *Focus on Autism and Other Developmental Disabilities*, 15, 12–20.

Connelly, M. (2004). *Children with autism: strategies for accessing the curriculum key stages 3&4*. Blackpool: North West Regional SEN Partnership.

Cumine, V., Dunlop, J. and Stevenson, G. (2010). *Asperger Syndrome: A practical guide for teachers*. 2nd edition. Abingdon: Routledge.

Dowd, S. (2010). *The London Eye Mystery*. London: David Fickling Books.

Dubin, N. (2007). *Asperger Syndrome and Bullying: Strategies and solutions*. London, Jessica Kingsley Publishers.

Duffy, F.H., Shankardass, A., McAnulty, G.B. and Al, A. (2013). The relationship of Asperger's syndrome to autism: a preliminary EEG coherence study. *BMC Medicine*, 11, 175.

Elvén, B.H. (2010). *No Fighting, No Biting, No Screaming. How to make behaving positively possible for people with autism and other developmental disabilities*. London: Jessica Kingsley Publishers.

Frith, U. (2003). *Autism: Explaining the enigma*. 2nd edition. Oxford: Wiley-Blackwell.

Frith, U. and Snowling, M. (1983). Reading for meaning and reading for sound in autistic and dyslexic children. *British Journal of Developmental Psychology*, 1(4), 329–342.

Gernsbacher, M.A. and Robertson, R. (1999). The role of suppression in figurative language comprehension. *Journal of Pragmatics*, 31, 1619–30.

Glenndenning, J. (Statistician). Statistical First Release, Key Stage 4 Attainment by Pupil Characteristics, in England (2008/2009). Retrieved 5 May 2012: www.education.gov.uk/rsgateway/DB/SFR/s000900/ index.shtml

Gold, R., Faust M. and Goldstein, A. (2010). Semantic integration during metaphor comprehension in Asperger syndrome. *Brain and Language*, 113, 124–134.

Griswold, D.E., Barnhill, G.P., Myles, B.S., Hagiwara, T. and Simpson, R. L. (2002). Asperger syndrome and academic achievement. *Focus on Autism and Other Developmental Disabilities*, 17, 94–102.

Haddon, M. (2004). *The Curious Incident of the Dog in the Night Time*. Children's Edition. Vintage Reprints.

Hala, S., Pexman, P.M. and Glenwright, M. (2007). Priming the meaning of homographs in typically developing children and children with autism. *Journal of Autism and Developmental Disorders*, 37, 329–340.

Happé, F. and Frith, U. (2006). The weak coherence account: detail-focused cognitive style in autism spectrum disorders. *Journal of Autism and Developmental Disorders*, 36(1), 5–25.

Henderson, L.M., Clarke, P.J. and Snowling, M.J. (2011). Accessing and selecting word meaning in autism spectrum disorder. *Journal of Child Psychology and Psychiatry*, 52(9), 964–973.

Hesmondhalgh, M. (2006). *Access and Inclusion on the Front Line*. London: Jessica Kingsley Publishers.

Huemer, S.V. and Mann, V. (2010). A comprehensive profile of decoding and comprehension in autism spectrum disorders. *Journal of Autism and Developmental Disorders*, 40, 485–493.

Humphrey, N. (2012). *Inclusion of Pupils with Autistic Spectrum Disorders in Mainstream Secondary Schools – Challenges and opportunities*. ESRC Impact Report, RES-061-25-0054. Swindon: ESRC.

Humphrey, N. and Symes, W. (2011). Peer interaction patterns among adolescents with autistic spectrum disorders (ASDs) in mainstream school settings. *Autism*, 15, 4.

Jackson, L. (2003). *Freaks, Geeks and Asperger Syndrome*. London, Jessica Kingsley Publishers.

Jolliffe, T. and Baron-Cohen, S. (1999). A test of central coherence theory: linguistic processing in high-functioning adults with autism or Asperger syndrome: Is local coherence impaired? *Cognition*, 71, 149–185.

Jones, G., English, A., Guldberg, K., Jordan, R., Richardson, P. and Waltz, M. (2009). *Educational Provision for Children and Young People on the Autism Spectrum Living in England: A review of current practice, issues and challenges*. Autism Centre for Education and Research, University of Birmingham.

Jung-Beeman, M. (2005). Bilateral brain processes for comprehending natural language. *Trends in Cognitive Sciences*, 9, 512–518.

Just, M. A., Cherkassky, V.L., Keller, T.A. and Minshew, N.J. (2004). Cortical activation and synchronization during sentence comprehension in high-functioning autism: evidence of underconnectivity. *Brain*, 127, 1811–1821.

Kaland, N., Møller-Nielsen, A., Smith, L., Mortensen, E.L., Callesen, K. and Gottlieb, D. (2005). The Strange Stories test. A replication study of children and adolescents with Asperger syndrome. *European Child and Adolescent Psychiatry*, 14, 73–82.

Lawson, W. (2000). *Life Behind Glass: A personal account of Autism Spectrum Disorder*. London: Jessica Kingsley Publishers.

—— (2011). *The Passionate Mind: How people with autism learn*. London: Jessica Kingsley Publishers.

Le Sourn-Bissaoui, S., Caillies, S., Gierski, F. and Motte, J. (2011). Ambiguity detection in adolescents with Asperger syndrome: is central coherence or theory of mind impaired? *Research in Autism Spectrum Disorders*, 5, 648–656.

Loukusa, S., Leinonen, E., Jussila, K., Mattila, M-L., Ryder, N., Ebeling, H. and Moilanen, I. (2007). Answering contextually demanding questions: pragmatic errors produced by children with Asperger syndrome or high functioning autism. *Journal of Communication Disorders*, 40, 357–381.

Lyons, V. and Fitzgerald, M. (2004). Humor in autism and Asperger syndrome. *Journal of Autism and Developmental Disorders*, 34(5), 521–532.

Markram, H., Rinaldi, T. and Markram, K. (2007). The Intense World Syndrome – an alternative hypothesis for autism. *Frontiers in Neuroscience* 1:1. Retrieved from www.frontiersin.org, 28 December 2013.

Martin, I. and McDonald, S. (2004). An exploration of causes of non-literal language problems in individuals with Asperger syndrome. *Journal of Autism and Developmental Disorders*, 34(3), 311–328.

Mashal, N., Faust, M., Hendler, T. and Jung-Beeman, M. (2008). Hemispheric differences in processing the literal interpretation of idioms: Converging evidence from behavioral and fMRI studies. *Cortex*, 10, 1016, 1–13.

Mashal, N. and Kasirer, A. (2012). Principal component analysis study of visual and verbal metaphoric comprehension in children with autism and learning disabilities. *Research in Developmental Disabilities*, 33, 274–282.

Morewood, G.D., Humphrey, N. and Symes, W. (2011). Mainstreaming autism: making it work. *Good Autism Practice*, 12(2), 62–68.

Myles, B.S. and Southwick, J. (2005). *Asperger Syndrome and Difficult Moments: Practical solutions for tantrums, rage and meltdowns*. 2nd revised edition. Kansas: Autism Asperger Publishing Co.

Myles, B.S., Cook, K.T., Miller, N.E., Rinner, L. and Robbins, L.A. (2005 reprint). *Asperger Syndrome and Sensory Issues: Practical solutions for making sense of the world*. Kansas: Autism Asperger Publishing Co.

Nation, K. and Norbury, C.F. (2005). Why reading comprehension fails insights from developmental disorders. *Topics in Language Disorders*, 25(1), 21–32.

Norbury, C.F. (2005). The relationship between theory of mind and metaphor: Evidence from children with language impairment and autistic spectrum disorder. *British Journal of Developmental Psychology*, 23, 383–399.

O'Connor, I.M. and Klein, P.D. (2004). Exploration of strategies for facilitating the reading comprehension of high-functioning students with autism spectrum disorders. *Journal of Autism and Developmental Disorders*, 34(2), 115–126.

Pellicano, E., Maybery, M., Durkin, K. and Maley, A. (2006). Multiple cognitive capabilities deficits in children with an autism spectrum disorder: 'Weak' central coherence and its relationship to theory of mind and executive control. *Development and Psychopathology*, 18, 77–98.

Picoult, J. (2010). *House Rules*. London: Hodder Paperbacks.

Priestley, J.B. (1945/2011). *An Inspector Calls – The Graphic Novel: Original Text*. [Paperback] Will Volley (Illustrator), Jason Cobley (Translator). Classical Comics.

Reid, B. and Batten, A. (2006). *B is for bullied: the experiences of children with autism and their families*. The National Autistic Society.

Riley-hall, E. (2012). *Parenting Girls on the Autism Spectrum: Overcoming the challenges and celebrating the gifts*. London: Jessica Kingsley Publishers.

Sainsbury, C. (2003). *Martian in the Playground*. London: Sage Publications Inc.

Saldaña, D. and Frith, U. (2007). Do readers with autism make bridging inferences from world knowledge? *Journal of Experimental Child Psychology*, 96, 310–319.

Saldaña, D., Carreiras, M. and Frith, U. (2009). Orthographic and phonological pathways in hyperlexic readers with autism spectrum disorders. *Developmental Neuropsychology*, 33(3), 240–253.

Shakespeare, W. (1606/2008). *Macbeth – The Graphic Novel: Original Text*. Unabridged. John McDonald (Adapter), Karen Wenborn (Collaborator), Nigel Dobbyn (Colorist), Jo Wheeler (Designer), Clive Bryant (Editor), Jon Haward (Illustrator), Gary Erskine (Illustrator). Classical Comics; British English edition.

Shelley, M. (1818/2008). *Frankenstein – The Graphic Novel: Original Text*. Jason Cobley (Adapter), Karen Wenborn (Collaborator), Jon Haward (Collaborator), Jason Cardy and Kat Nicholson (Colourist), Jenny Placentino (Compiler), Jo Wheeler (Designer), Clive Bryant (Editor), Declan Shalvey (Illustrator), Terry Wiley (Illustrator). Classical Comics; British English edition.

Silver, K. (2005). *Assessing and Developing Communication and Thinking Skills in People with Autism and Communication Difficulties. A toolkit for parents and professionals*. London: Jessica Kingsley Publishers.

Simone, R. (2010). *Aspergirls. Empowering Females with Asperger Syndrome*. London: Jessica Kingsley Publishers.

Songlee, D., Miller, S.P., Tincani, M., Sileo, N.M. and Perkins, P.G. (2008). Effects of test-taking strategy instruction on high-functioning adolescents with autism spectrum disorders. *Focus on Autism and Other Developmental Disabilities*, 23, 217–228.

Steinbeck, J. (1965). *Of Mice and Men*. Oxford: New Windmill Series.

Supekar, K., Uddin, L.Q., Khouzam, A., Phillips, J., Gaillard, W.D., Kenworthy, L.E., Yerys, B.E., Vaidya, C.J. and Menon, V. (2013). Brain Hyperconnectivity in Children with Autism and its Links to Social Deficits. Cell Press Open Access. Retrieved from http://download.cell.com/cell-reports/mmcs/journals/2211-1247/PIIS2211124713005706.mmc2.pdf on 16 November 2013.

Tager-Flusberg, H. and Joseph, R.M. (2003). Identifying neurocognitive phenotypes in autism. *Philosophical Transactions of the Royal Society of London B: Biological Sciences*, 358, 303–314.

Tager-Flusberg, H., Paul, R. and Lord, C. (2005). Language and communication in autism. In F. Volkmar, R. Paul, A. Klin, and D.J. Cohen (eds), *Handbook of Autism and Pervasive Developmental Disorders*. 3rd edition. New York: Wiley.

Tammet, D. (2007). *Born on a Blue Day: The gift of an extraordinary mind*. London: Hodder Paperback.

Tesink, C.M.J.Y., Buitelaar, J.K., Petersson, K.M., van der Gaag, R.J., Teunisse, J-P. and Hagoort, P. (2011). Neural correlates of language comprehension in autism spectrum disorders: when language conflicts with world knowledge. *Neuropsychologia*, 49, 1095–1104.

Virtue, S., Parrish, T. and Jung-Beeman, M. (2008). Inferences during Story C comprehension: cortical recruitment affected by predictability of events and working memory capacity. *Journal of Cognitive Neuroscience*, 20(12), 2274–2284.

Wahlberg, T. and Magliano, J.P. (2004). The ability of high function individuals with autism to comprehend written discourse. *Discourse Processes*, 38(1), 119–144.

Wearing, C. (2010). Autism, metaphor and relevance theory. *Mind and Language*, 25(2), 196–216.

WHO (2007). *International Classification of Diseases and Related Health Problems*. Tenth Edition (ICD-10). Geneva: World Health Organization.

Wilkinson, K. and Twist, L. (2010). *Autism and educational assessment: UK policy and practice*. Slough: NFER. Retrieved 2 August 2011 from www.nfer.ac.uk/nfer/publications/ASR02/ASR02.pdf

Wing, L. (1996, 2002). *The Autistic Spectrum*. New updated edition. London: Robinson.

Wing. L. and Shah, A. (2000). Catatonia in autistic spectrum disorders. *British Journal of Psychiatry*, 176, 357–362. Downloaded from http://bjp.rcpsych.org/ on 24 March 2013. Published by The Royal College of Psychiatrists.

Internet pages

ABC Analysis: www.specialconnections.ku.edu/?q=behavior_plans/functional_behavior_assessment/teacher_tools/antecedent_behavior_consequence_chart

Autism Education Trust: www.aettraininghubs.org.uk/wp-content/uploads/2012/06/AET-National-Autism-Standards_distributed.pdf

Communicate In Print 2: www.widgit.com

Drama: http://dramaresource.com

Graphic Novels: www.classicalcomics.com

Maps: www.freeusandworldmaps.com/html/WorldRegions/WorldRegionsPrint.html

Paley, S. (2013). Seclusion Rooms: A parents' guide. www.downssideup.com/2013/01/seclusion-rooms-parents-guide.html

Social Stories and Comic Conversations: Carol Gray https://www.thegraycenter.org

Stanislavsky System: https://www.theatrefolk.com/spotlights/the-stanislavsky-system

www.secondarymathsite.co.uk/Literacy%20in%20Mathematics.html

Facebook pages

Autism Discussion Page by Bill Nason, Psychologist. Describing, explaining and offering strategies to assist supporting children on the spectrum. https://www.facebook.com/autismdiscussionpage?fref=ts

YouTube videos

A Child's View of Sensory Processing – ESGWNRM www.youtube.com/watch?v=D1G5ssZlVUw

A is for Autism, BBC Four: www.youtube.com/watch?v=cPR2H4Zd8bl

BBC Newsround – My Autism and Me: Rosie www.youtube.com/watch?v=ejpWWP1HNGQ

Daniel Tammet: The Boy with the Incredible Brain

Dean Beadle – an extract from his talk in Cardiff in which he describes his impulsive behaviour – running away from his mother in a supermarket with the shopping trolley in his 20s. Very funny and illustrates the lack of self-control. Will need editing. www.youtube.com/watch?v=LC0JytWaQZM

Derek Paravacini: Musical Genius

Sensory Overload Simulation – WeirdGirlCyndi www.youtube.com/watch?v=BPDTEuotHe0

Stephen Wiltshire draws a picture of Rome in 3 days: Beautiful Minds

www.sensory-processing-disorder.com/

Film

Lurhman B. (Director), *Romeo and Juliet* (1996). Bazmark Films, Twentieth Century Fox Film Corporation.

Sinise, G. (Director), *Of Mice and Men* (1992). United States: Metro Goldwyn Meyer.

Zeffirelli, F. (Director), *Romeo and Juliet* (1968). BHE Films, Verona Produzione, Dino de Laurentiis Cinematografica.

Art

David, J. L., 'Napoleon Crossing the Alps on 20th May, 1800'.

Delaroche, P., 'Napoleon Crossing the Alps'. St James' Palace, London.

Levine, D., 1964. 'Napoleon Crossing the Alps'. The New York Review of Books, June 25, 1964 • Vol 2, No 10. Reproduced with the generous permission of the artist's son and daughter.

Index